There's a Stat for That!

The most important person in my life is my wife, Bonnie Johnson.
She is always the variable upon which I depend. (See what I did there?)

There's a Stat for That!

What to Do & When to Do It

Bruce B. Frey

University of Kansas

Los Angeles | London | New Delhi
Singapore | Washington DC | Boston

Los Angeles | London | New Delhi
Singapore | Washington DC | Boston

FOR INFORMATION:

SAGE Publications, Inc.

2455 Teller Road

Thousand Oaks, California 91320

E-mail: order@sagepub.com

SAGE Publications Ltd.

1 Oliver's Yard

55 City Road

London EC1Y 1SP

United Kingdom

SAGE Publications India Pvt. Ltd.

B 1/I 1 Mohan Cooperative Industrial Area

Mathura Road, New Delhi 110 044

India

SAGE Publications Asia-Pacific Pte. Ltd.

3 Church Street

#10-04 Samsung Hub

Singapore 049483

Copyright © 2016 by SAGE Publications, Inc.

Printed in the United States of America

Cataloging-in-Publication Data is available for this title from the Library of Congress.

ISBN 978-1-4833-1875-2

This book is printed on acid-free paper.

Acquisitions Editor: Vicki Knight

Editorial Assistant: Yvonne McDuffee

Associate Editor: Katie Bierach

Production Editor: Kelly DeRosa

Copy Editor: Mark Bast

Typesetter: C&M Digitals (P) Ltd.

Proofreader: Jennifer Grubba

Indexer: Michael Ferreira

Cover Designer: Michael Dubowe

Marketing Manager: Nicole Elliott

SUSTAINABLE FORESTRY INITIATIVE

Certified Chain of Custody
Promoting Sustainable Forestry
www.sfiprogram.org
SFI-01268

SFI label applies to text stock

15 16 17 18 19 10 9 8 7 6 5 4 3 2 1

Contents

There's a Stat for That!

What to do. When to do it.

Check out **The Basics** for definitions of all the jargon used in these questions.

1. How many independent and dependent variables do you have?

2. Are your variables at the nominal, ordinal, or interval level (or above)?

3. How many levels do your variables have?

4. How many groups of people (or things) are you including in your analysis?

5. What is the number of measurement occasions in your design?

Locate the answers to these questions on the following big fun table. It will point you to the right *Stat for That!*

Frequency Analyses

Independent Variables				Dependent Variables			Number of Measurement Occasions	Stat for That!	Page
Number	Level of Measurement	Number of Levels	Number of Groups	Number	Level of Measurement	Number of Levels			
0	—	—	1	1	Nominal	2	1	1. Binomial Test	10
0	—	—	1	1	Nominal	2+	1	2. Chi-Squared	12
0	—	—	1	1	Ordinal	Many	1	3. Kolmogorov-Smirnov Test	14
0	—	—	1	1	Interval	Many	1	4. Single-Sample t Test	16
1	Nominal	2	1	1	Nominal	2	1	5. Fisher Exact Test	18
1	Nominal	2+	1	1	Nominal	2+	1	6. Two-Way Chi-Squared	20

| Group Comparisons | | | | | | | | | |
| Independent Variables | | | | Dependent Variables | | | | | |
Number	Level of Measurement	Number of Levels	Number of Groups	Number	Level of Measurement	Number of Levels	Number of Measurement Occasions	Stat for That!	Page
1	Nominal	2	2	1	Ordinal	2	1	7. Mann-Whitney Test	24
1	Nominal	2	2	1	Interval	Many	1	8. Independent t Test	26
1	Nominal	2+	2+	1	Ordinal	Many	1	9. Median Test	28
1	Nominal	2+	2+	1	Ordinal	Many	1	10. Kruskal-Wallis Test	30
1	Nominal	2+	2+	1	Interval	Many	1	11. Analysis of Variance	32
2	Nominal	2+	2+	1	Interval	Many	1	12. Two-Way Analysis of Variance	34
1	Nominal	2+	2+	1	Interval	Many	1	13. Analysis of Covariance	36
1	Nominal	2+	2+	2+	Interval	Many	1	14. Multivariate Analysis of Variance	38

Repeated Measures Analyses

Independent Variables				Dependent Variables			Number of Measurement Occasions	Stat for That!	Page
Number	Level of Measurement	Number of Levels	Number of Groups	Number	Level of Measurement	Number of Levels			
1	Nominal	2	1	1	Nominal	2+	2	15. McNemar Change Test	42
1	Nominal	2	1	1	Ordinal	2+	2	16. Wilcoxon Signed Ranks Test	44
1	Nominal	2	1	1	Interval	Many	2	17. Paired-Samples t Test	46
1	Nominal	2+	1	1	Nominal	2+	2+	18. Cochran Q Test	48
1	Nominal	2+	1	1	Ordinal	2+	2+	19. Friedman Test	50
1	Nominal	2+	1	1	Interval	Many	2+	20. Repeated Measures Analysis of Variance	52
2+	Nominal	2+	1	1	Interval	Many	2+	21. Two-Way Repeated Measures	54
2+	Nominal	2+	2+	1	Interval	Many	2+	22. Mixed Analysis of Variance	56
1	Nominal	Many	1	1	Interval	Many	2+	23. Time Series Analysis	58

Correlational Analyses

Predictor Variables			Number of Groups	Criterion Variables			Number of Measurement Occasions	Stat for That!	Page
Number	Level of Measurement	Number of Levels		Number	Level of Measurement	Number of Levels			
0	—	—	1	1	Nominal	2+	2+	24. Kappa Coefficient of Agreement	62
1	Ordinal	Many	1	1	Ordinal	Many	1	25. Spearman Correlation Coefficient	64
1	Nominal	2	1	1	Nominal	2	1	26. Phi Correlation Coefficient	66
1	Nominal	2+	1	1	Nominal	2+	1	27. Cramér's V Coefficient	68
1	Nominal+	2+	1	1	Nominal	2	1	28. Simple Logistic Regression	70
2+	Nominal+	2+	1	1	Nominal	2	1	29. Multiple Logistic Regression	72
1	Nominal+	2+	1	1	Nominal	2+	1	30. Discriminant Analysis	74
1	Interval	Many	1	1	Interval	Many	1	31. Pearson Correlation Coefficient	76
1	Interval	Many	1	1	Interval	Many	1	32. Simple Linear Regression	78
2+	Interval	Many	1	1	Interval	Many	1	33. Multiple Linear Regression	80
2+	Interval	Many	1	2+	Interval	Many	1	34. Canonical Correlation	82
2+	Interval	Many	1	2+	Interval	Many	1	35. Exploratory Factor Analysis	84
2+	Interval	Many	1	2+	Interval	Many	1	36. Confirmatory Factor Analysis	86
2+	Interval	Many	1	2+	Interval	Many	1	37. Cluster Analysis	88
You wish to analyze a chain of correlations among several interval level variables.								38. Path Analysis	90
You wish to analyze a set of correlational chains and theoretical unmeasured variables.								39. Structural Equation Modeling	92
You wish to control for the fact that your data are not independent of each other.								40. Hierarchical Linear Modeling	94

Preface

It might seem strange to offer a statistics book that doesn't tell you how to do statistics. Even odder, perhaps, is how proudly we point that out and how the promotional material for this book even emphasizes the fact! But, you see, many books, websites, and professors and teachers do a dandy job of teaching statistics, in terms of the steps and procedures for analyzing data and interpreting the results. In my experience, though, and (my guess is) in the experience of many, the field doesn't do a very good job of explaining *why* the particular statistical approach is the right one to use and, often, even *which* particular statistical approach is the right one to use for a given research design. Experts, like your stats professor and the authors of textbooks, are able to analyze a research design and know based on some mysterious characteristics of the design that you should use *multiple linear regression*, or a *Friedman test*, or *multivariate analysis of variance*, or whatever.

This book reveals the mysterious characteristics that determine the right stat to use. It turns out (spoiler alert!) that it is the *number of independent and dependent variables* and the *level of measurement* of those variables that pretty much determine the right statistic to use. (By the way, if you've forgotten that jargon, or were never really taught what that all means, don't worry, we'll bring you up to speed in "The Basics" chapter.) So, this book describes dozens of research designs in terms of number of variables and their levels of measurement and the dozens of statistical procedures that match up with those designs. In fact, using the unique big fun table of procedures in the front of the book, you can look up any design using these characteristics and be pointed to a concise two-page description of the procedure that outlines what you need to know about how it's used and why it's the appropriate analytic strategy, a real-world study that has used it, how the data is analyzed, and how results are interpreted. Plus, you get all sorts of other things to keep in mind when using that procedure. What the description *doesn't* do, as I proudly proclaimed at the beginning, is tell you *how* to do the analysis. This book "only" tells you about *which* stat to use and *why* that's the stat to use.

So, if you're a consultant, or writing a grant proposal, or collaborating with others on a research project, or a student trying to figure out the secret ways of experts, or able to access resources to help you do the stats once you know which stat to use, this book is designed for you. Because there *is* a right answer, you know. No matter what the quantitative design or nature of the research question, just figure out the variables and how they are measured, and, rest assured, there is a stat for that!

Bruce Frey
October 2014

Acknowledgments

Many people have helped create *There's a Stat for That!*

First, this project would never have existed without the support and guidance of my editor at SAGE, Vicki Knight. I'm grateful that she liked the idea when she first heard it (she *got it* right away), and I am lucky that she bought in to the idea that there was a need for a radically different kind of statistics book. She also has done her job well as an editor and is the best with whom I've ever worked.

Second, an invaluable assistant for this book was Zachery Conrad. He is responsible for the diversity and interesting nature of the many real-world examples discussed here. If you are pleased to find an example of a study from your particular narrow area of interest, it is thanks to Zach. (I call him Zach, that's how close we are.)

Finally, there are the usual suspects when it comes to acknowledging guiding forces behind what I write. Professionally, Neil Salkind has been a mentor for writing books like this. I have learned much under him.

Regarding production of this book, I want to thank the large group of reviewers, statistics professors all, who provided patient and detailed feedback throughout this process. I've incorporated almost all of their advice! They include the following:

Joel S. Steele, *Portland State University*

Nicole McDonald, *Cornerstone University*

Linda Martinez, *California State University–Long Beach*

Joe Benz, *University of Nebraska at Kearney*

Yeonsoo Kim, *University of Nevada Las Vegas*

T. John Alexander, *Texas Wesleyan University*

Mark W. Tengler, *University of Houston–Clear Lake*

Matthew D. Dean, *University of Southern Maine*

Stella G. Lopez, *University of Texas at San Antonio*

This book wouldn't have looked as nice if not for these editors and production folks at SAGE:

Mark Bast

Kelly DeRosa

Michael Ferreira

Jennifer Grubba

Thanks everyone!

About the Author

Bruce B. Frey, PhD, is an award-winning teacher and scholar at the University of Kansas. His areas of research include classroom assessment and instrument development. Dr. Frey is the author of *Statistics Hacks*, published by O'Reilly, and SAGE publications *Modern Classroom Assessment* (2013) and *100 Questions (and Answers) About Tests and Measurement* (2014). He also is the coeditor of SAGE's *Encyclopedia of Research Design*. In his spare time, he collects comic books and is especially fond of 1960s DC stories wherein superpets turn against their superhero masters.

The Basics

How This Book Works

Near the front of this book is a big fun table that lists forty statistical procedures. This functions as a guide, a detailed second table of contents of sorts, where you can identify the characteristics of your research design and find the right statistic for your use. Turn to the right page and you'll find a brief description of the right procedure for your research question and when it should be used. You'll also get a sense of the logic behind the analysis and how it works. The big fun table tells you *what to do* and *when to do it*.

The analyses are organized into four groups based on their purpose: *frequency analysis*, *group comparisons*, *repeated measures analyses*, and *correlational analyses*. Within each group, the analyses are sequenced based on the level of measurement for the *independent* and *dependent* variables (or, for correlational analyses, *predictor* and *criterion* variables) and their complexity in terms of the number of variables involved.

What This Book Doesn't Do

This is an odd sort of statistics book. It doesn't teach you how to *do* statistics. Nothing here explains how to actually *do* an analysis, either by hand with calculations or on a computer using software. The thing is, there are plenty of textbooks, software manuals and help menus, websites, and stats teachers that do a pretty good job of teaching how to *do* statistical analyses, and we don't need another book for that. What is sometimes missing from those books and college classes, though, is learning *which* statistic to use. If you are told to perform a paired-samples *t* test, you might be able to do that fairly well. But *when* should you use a paired-samples *t* test? And why? How about more complex analyses like multiple logistic regression or multivariate analysis of variance? Even if students or PhDs might be able to perform those analyses with the help of your notes, textbooks, software, professors, or consultants, the field of statistics doesn't always do a great job of making it clear which of the many possible statistical analyses one should use for a given research design.

This book is designed to fill that gap between theory and practice. Whether you are a student, professor, researcher, or grant proposal writer, we assume that you have other sources for actually *doing* the analysis, but you need to know which one to do. And in most cases there is a right one to choose. No matter what your design, no matter what your research question, rest assured, there is a stat for that.

Though I've tried hard to avoid as much jargon and technical language as possible in this book, a shared understanding of several key concepts and terms will provide a helpful foundation for what's to come. Here are the basics, starting with *the* most important concept.

Level of Measurement

The abstract variables that researchers evaluate can usually be quantified in a variety of ways. The rules by which numbers are assigned to represent those variables determine their *level of measurement*. Different levels of measurement provide different amounts of information about variables and correspond to different sets of statistical procedures that make sense. Consequently, it is the level of measurement used for a given set of research variables that almost always determines which statistical analysis to use.

Nominal

Nominal comes from a Latin word meaning "in name only" and describes the lowest level of measurement where numbers are used, but only as names for different categories. For instance, social science researchers often assign *1's* and *2's* for the variable of sex: a *1* might mean *male* and a *2* might mean *female*. These *1's* and *2's* are still scores, but it doesn't make sense to treat them as quantities. Female is not twice as much as male.

Ordinal

Providing a bit more information than the nominal level, at this level, the scores represent some rank order. Regardless of which variable is being measured, the scores indicate *more* or *less* of something. We can distinguish between scores, but because we don't know what the distances are between the different ranks, we can't even summarize how much variance the group has.

Interval

At this level, we have the ranking information as at the ordinal level, but now the scoring rules are such that the spacing between scores reflects equal *amounts* of the variable. Think of a thermometer where the amount of heat between 25 and 30 degrees is the same amount of heat found between 30 and 35 degrees. Because we must be at the interval level to meaningfully calculate the average known as the *mean*, and so many useful statistical tests make use of means, many researchers try to measure their variables at this level.

Ratio

The fourth, and highest, level of measurement differs from the interval level only in that negative values are not allowed. One cannot have less than 0 of ratio level variables. Think of ratio level measurement as a simple count of something like money or inches or dogs on a porch. At the interval level, one could use a scale with negative numbers (think of temperatures below 0, for example), but not at this level. That rule allows for one more type of analysis to be used (comparing values to each other using proportions or ratios) but is only a slight improvement over interval level measurement. So, instead of treating ratio level measurement as the goal for good research, we usually speak of "interval or above," and this book only refers to nominal, ordinal, and interval levels.

Identifying Your Level of Measurement

Nominal

If a variable is really just a bunch of categories (e.g., groups to compare, sex, political party, personality type, location), it is at the nominal level. In fact, statisticians often refer to nominal variables as *categorical variables*. All those statistics that compare group means to each other, like *t* tests and analyses of variance? They have nominal independent variables.

Ordinal

Variables measured above the nominal level are sometimes called *continuous variables*. That's because the scores represent some sort of quantity with a range of values somewhere along a continuum from less of the quantity to more of the quantity. All continuous variables, at the very least, are ordinal. The scores reflect some order on that continuum. If the assigned scores aren't able to capture equal chunks along that continuum, they *only* reflect their order.

Interval

Continuous variables that not only reflect some order but have scores assigned in a way where the distance between any two adjacent scores represents an equal amount of that variable are interval level variables. If this is hard to picture in a way that makes sense, compare interval level to ordinal level to see how much more information is available. Beyond the interval level thermometer example, think of all those psychological, educational, and attitudinal tests and surveys that produce a total score that is the combination of responses to many questions. Those scores represent much more than a simple indication of the rank ordering on whatever variable is being measured. Even if it is not clear that each interval between scores is equal all along the full range of scores, most researchers treat scores from measures like these as interval level variables.

Interval or Ordinal?

It may be hard for a researcher to decide if a continuous variable is at the interval level or "only" ordinal. Sometimes even statisticians disagree about what to do in these situations. In fact, the idea earlier that "all those psychological, educational, and attitudinal tests and surveys that produce a total score that is the combination of responses to many questions" are at the interval level is not accepted by some and, strictly speaking, isn't even a true statement. Fortunately, the debate is mainly an academic one because, in most cases, even if a continuous variable that is more than ordinal level doesn't meet the technical specifications of being truly at the interval level, we can treat it *as if* it is interval. All the statistics that require interval level variables work pretty well for these "almost" interval level variables, too. This is especially true if the score in question is a combination of many such questionable scores. That's because these total scores tend to distribute themselves in the same way as truly interval level scores do. And the right statistic to use is all about the expected distribution of those scores in a population.

So, when in doubt, why not decide that you're at the lower level of measurement and not worry about things? After all, the statistics that work for ordinal variables will also work for interval variables. The goal, though, is to measure each variable in a way that captures as much information as possible and to use the most powerful statistical procedures available. And the most powerful statistical procedures are those that use interval level variables.

Independent and Dependent Variables

Many research hypotheses suggest that one variable affects another. In those hypotheses, the variable that is affected by the other is labeled the *dependent variable* because it depends on the other variable. The variable doing the affecting, the supposed causal variable, is called the *independent variable*. Certainly, in the broader real world, all sorts of variables are affecting that independent variable, but those variables aren't part of this particular hypothesis, so we call it the independent variable.

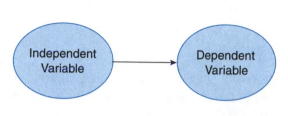

Predictor and Criterion Variables

Instead of suggesting that one variable affects another, some hypotheses suppose only that variables are related to each other (or, as statisticians say, *correlated*). Because there is no cause-and-effect relationship explicitly stated in these hypotheses, it is not correct to label one variable *independent* and another variable *dependent*. (Strangely, many popular statistical software applications insist on labeling their correlational variables in this way.) Often, even in a correlational study, however, there is some direction in the relationships implied. We may use correlations to see whether one variable *explains* another, for example, or use several variables to *predict* another. In those cases, we distinguish between the roles of variables in the design by using the term *predictor variable* for the one that is kind of "independenty" and *criterion variable* for the one we are trying to explain or predict. Of course, with a simple correlation between two variables, we don't need to give them different labels because the relationship might not have any direction involved in it.

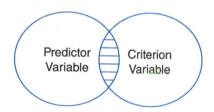

Score

A score is the general term for the number assigned to represent a research participant's placement on a variable. Depending on the level of measurement, it can represent which category people are in, people's relative order compared to each other, people's score on a measure, and so on. Statisticians sometimes call scores *observations* to remind us that scores represent a sample of possible scores. As such, there was some sort of chance involved in their presence in a study. It is the influence of chance on these scores that requires (and allows for) inferential statistical analysis.

Level

A *level* is a possible score on a variable. If a nominal variable has three categories, it has three levels. An interval variable with scores ranging from 40 to 160 has 121 levels.

Group

A *group* means a group of participants. Sometimes, statistical analyses compare several groups of people to each other (e.g., analysis of variance). Sometimes, statistical analyses compare several groups of scores that have been collected from one group of participants (e.g., repeated measures). When the term *group* is used in the opening summary of each statistic and in the big fun table at the front of the book, it means the *groups of participants* that provided scores for analysis.

Participants

Participants is the word used in this book for the unit of analysis that provides the scores we discuss. Participants are the subjects of a study. The statistical analyses described in this book work for studies involving things, too, of course, such as gravel, otters, and radio waves. For simplicity's sake, in this book I'll usually assume that the participants in these research designs are people, but they need not be. The analyses don't know or care where their data came from.

Statistic

Technically, a statistic is a quantitative value that describes the scores in a sample. In practice, the term *statistics* is used more loosely to describe the whole field of statistical analysis. It is often used to describe the process, not the actual sample value tested for significance. For example, *analysis of variance* is sometimes referred to as a statistic, when it is actually an analytic strategy that produces an *F* value. The *F* is the statistic, not the analysis of variance. This book uses both senses of the term *statistic*.

Types of Statistics

This book groups forty statistical analyses into four categories or types of analyses.

Frequency analysis is used when one is interested in the distribution of one or more variables in a single sample. Does the pattern of scores seem to be due to chance or something else? These designs usually involve nominal level variables and often have no independent variable.

Group comparisons are analyses that compare groups to each other. Like traditional experimental designs (where an *experimental group* is compared to a *control group*), the independent variable in a group comparison is always nominal and the different levels are the different groups.

Repeated measures analyses use data from groups that have been measured more than once, usually on the same variable. Longitudinal designs almost always use repeated measures analyses. The comparisons are usually across time.

Correlational analyses involve one group of participants that have been measured on more than one variable. These analyses are usually interested in relationships among variables, not differences between groups or across time. In complex correlational analyses, though, group differences and changes across time can be included as variables to be analyzed.

"By Chance"

Explanations of statistical analyses almost always throw around the phrase "by chance." You hear it all the time: "Do the means differ more than would be expected by chance?" or "That's a bigger correlation than you'd find by chance" or "I conclude that these results did not occur by chance." It's important to be clear on which "chance" is being referred to in these conversations. It is not the type of chance that relates to gambling or winning the lottery or getting struck by lightning or getting lucky on a pop quiz in school. It is a specific type of chance that applies to statistical analyses. Because inferential statistics are trying to guess population values by examining sample values, they rely on their samples representing the population accurately. If researchers' samples do not represent their populations well, their statistical conclusions will be wrong. (This is why random selection of a sample from the larger population is so important.) Bad luck in statistical analysis means you have a sample that does not reflect the population well in terms of the statistical value about which you are speculating. A sample is not made up of all the scores in a population, so we expect some small difference in our sample values compared to the population values. If the sample is selected randomly, however, we would only expect a small difference. *By chance* alone, we would expect a small difference. Statisticians know how big that small difference should be. If the difference between a sample value and some hypothesized population value is bigger than would be expected *by chance* alone, they declare the difference to be statistically significant. By definition, it is significant because it is more different than would be expected *by chance*.

Does Choosing the Right Statistic Really *Only* Depend on Levels of Measurement?

No. Almost, but no. There are occasionally times when the level of measurement dictates a particular statistical analysis, but a researcher decides that one or more assumptions for that statistic have not been met. An *assumption* is a characteristic of the variables or the research design that must be true in order to trust the mathematical accuracy of the level of significance (the p value) that is calculated. If one violates an assumption, one cannot be sure that the decision regarding statistical significance is correct. Because statistical analyses designed for the lower levels of measurement (*nominal* and *ordinal*) have fewer assumptions and assumptions that are easy to meet, researchers will occasionally switch from an interval level statistic to a lower-level one. In *all* cases, though, the statistical analyses suggested in this book will be the right place to start, and in *almost all* cases, it will be the right statistic to use. It really is as simple as that.

PART 1

FREQUENCY ANALYSIS

The statistical analyses in this Frequency Analysis section compare the distribution of some variable in a sample with some hypothesized or expected distribution. Are the frequencies of each score on a variable what you'd expect to find if random chance was the only explanation for results?

Only one of these analyses is interested in the relationship between variables, the **two-way chi-squared test** (see Module 6) or contingency analysis. The rest test hypotheses about distributions. You could think of the two-way chi-squared test as a correlational analysis, but because it is a logical extension of the **chi-squared test** (see Module 2) it makes sense to put it in this section.

Only one of the statistics in this section is *parametric*, the **single-sample *t* test** (see Module 4). The rest are *nonparametric*. A parameter is a value that describes a population of scores (as opposed to a *statistic*, which describes a sample of scores), and a parametric statistic is a procedure that makes some assumptions about the population from which a sample is chosen. The key assumption of parametric statistics is that the variables are normally distributed (in that familiar bell-curve shape) in the population from which they are sampled. This assumption of normal distribution allows one to use the mean of a group of scores in the analysis instead of counting every score. Even though the single-sample *t* test uses the mean of scores, and not the frequency of scores, it is here because, like the rest of the analyses in this section, it is not interested in the relationship between variables.

Binomial Test

Independent Variables	0
Level of Measurement	——
Number of Levels	——
Number of Groups	——
Dependent Variables	1
Level of Measurement	Nominal
Number of Levels	2
Measurement Occasions	1

Research Design

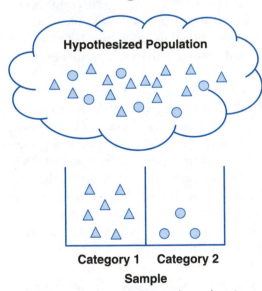

Hypothesized Population

Category 1   Category 2
Sample
Are the sample percentages in each category as expected?

The binomial test is the statistical analysis to use when there is a single nominal outcome variable of interest (the dependent variable) and there are only two possible scores for that variable (it is *dichotomous*). Those two values will distribute themselves in a given sample with one percentage of scores in one category and another percentage of scores in the other. These percentages will add up to 100%. Stated as proportions, the proportions will always sum to 1.0. The binomial test compares those sample proportions to some hypothesized or assumed proportions. Those proportions are often .50 and .50 (as one would expect with a flipped coin, for example), but they need not be. Data are collected from one group of people or things and the proportions in the sample are compared to hypothesized proportions.

Primary Statistical Question

Are my sample proportions different from what I expect?

Example of a Study That Would Use The Binomial Test

In the mountain villages of Peru, some children love asking riddles. These are the old-fashioned kind of "What am I?" riddles such as "I am a well-dressed lady in a yellow dress running around from corner to corner. What am I?" The answer is *a broom* (of course). A researcher noticed that these riddles usually involve social contexts of work and responsibility and hypothesized that responsible children would probably tend to like riddles. For the dependent variable, an interview method was developed that could place all children into one of two riddle affection categories: *likes riddles* or *does not like riddles*. It was determined in an earlier study that for all the mountain children, 60% like riddles. This was used as the expected proportion for the binomial test. A sample of 36 responsible children was selected (also determined through interviews). They were interviewed and scored on the dependent variable.

Analysis

Imagine that the data looked like this.

Dependent Variable	Frequency	Proportion
Likes riddles	28	.78
Does not like riddles	8	.22

In this case, the observed proportion was .78, which (with this sample size) is statistically larger than .60 (at the .02 level of significance). In this population, responsible children do tend to like riddles more than children in general.

Things to Consider

- The binomial test, and most of the other *frequency analysis* statistics, is described in this book as having no independent variables in its design. There is, of course, almost always some theoretical cause imagined as the explanation for whatever distribution of scores is being analyzed. In that sense, there *are* independent variables considered in the discussion of things. Independent variables do not provide scores for the analyses, however.
- A **chi-squared** test with just two categories could be used instead of the binomial test. In most cases, however, you will get slightly different levels of significance. This is because there are different assumptions made about how to calculate the probabilities with these procedures. For sample sizes of less than 100 or so, the binomial test is likely more accurate, but in most real-life situations, it won't matter which approach is used.
- The term *binomial* means two names, or two categories, or two possible values. The "nom" part of the word means "name" in the same way that "nom" is used in nominal level of measurement. In practice, we use the term *dichotomous* to mean the same thing as binomial, though, technically, *dichotomous* means "cut into two parts."

Real-Life Study That Inspired This Example

Bolton, R. (1977). Riddling and responsibility in highland Peru. *American Ethnologist, 4*(3), 497–516.

Chi-Squared

Independent Variables	0
Level of Measurement	——
Number of Levels	——
Number of Groups	——
Dependent Variables	1
Level of Measurement	Nominal
Number of Levels	2+
Measurement Occasions	1

Research Design

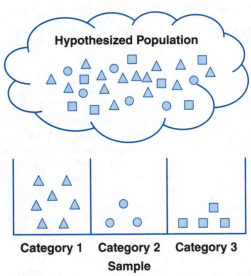

Hypothesized Population

Category 1   Category 2   Category 3

Sample

Is the frequency in each category as expected?

Chi-squared is the statistical analysis to use when there is a single nominal outcome variable of interest (the dependent variable) and there are more than two possible scores for that variable. Data are collected from one group of people or things and are scored on the dependent variable. In a given sample, different proportions will fall into each of the possible categories (or scores) for the dependent variable. The chi-squared test compares the frequencies in each category to what is hypothesized or expected. Often the assumed distribution is that all the categories will be equal and that there is no difference in the number of people at each level, but one can compare the sample against any expected proportions.

Primary Statistical Question

Are the frequencies in each level of the dependent variable different from what I expect?

Example of a Study That Would Use Chi-Squared

The manager of a local community theater wonders about the age of its season ticket holders. Are they young, middle-aged, or old? If one age range predominates, then that could guide the choice of productions toward the types of shows that the majority age range prefers. If age is roughly evenly distributed, though, then there is no need to use age as a reason for picking which plays to do. A survey of 141 season ticket holders was conducted, and among other demographic variables, *age* was collected. Age is the dependent variable in this study and it was scored using these categories: 18–44 = young, 45–64 = middle-aged, 65–93 = senior.

Analysis

Imagine that the results of the analysis looked like this.

Dependent Variable	Observed Frequency	Expected Frequency	Residual
Young	58	47	11
Middle-aged	52	47	5
Senior	31	47	−16

Observed frequency is the number of people in the sample that are in each category. *Expected frequency* is the number one would expect if there was no difference in the population represented by the sample (e.g., 141/3 = 47, so if age is equally distributed, we'd "expect" 47 in each category). *Residual* is the difference between the expected and actual frequencies. When those residuals add up to a big enough number, the chi-square computed from those residuals is statistically significant. Here, the chi-squared was 8.55, significance was $p = .01$, and the theater owner concluded that there were more young people and fewer seniors who owned season tickets. The next season there was more *Lion King* and less *South Pacific*.

Things to Consider

- Chi-squared, pronounced "Kye squared," is so named because of the statistical value the analysis produces and the Greek letter symbol that represents it, χ^2 It is one of those analyses named for the value that is tested for significance, like a *t* **test**, not for the strategy used, like **multiple linear regression** or **analysis of variance**.
- Chi-squared is more formally called the *chi-squared goodness-of-fit test*. How "good" do the observed proportions in your sample fit your hypothesis?
- *Chi-squared* is often referred to as *chi-square*. Mathematicians seem to be okay with this.
- Chi-squared is the statistic to use when you have a categorical (nominal) variable and you wish to declare that for a population of people, one category has the *most* or *least* in it.
- When there are only two categories in the dependent variable, a chi-squared test can still be used, but the **binomial test**, which is designed for exactly two categories, is usually a bit more accurate.
- The more categories (levels of the dependent variable) in the analysis, the easier it is for any differences between the observed and expected frequencies (those *residuals*) to add up to something statistically significant, even if it isn't really important. For a fairer chi-squared test, researchers sometimes collapse many categories into fewer, but still meaningful, categories. They also like to have at least 5 people in each category.

Kolmogorov-Smirnov Test

Independent Variables	0
Level of Measurement	——
Number of Levels	——
Number of Groups	1
Dependent Variables	1
Level of Measurement	Ordinal
Number of Levels	Many
Measurement Occasions	1

Research Design

A Kolmogorov-Smirnov test looks at the frequency of occurrences across a set of categories and compares the observed distribution to some theoretical expected distribution. The logic works for the probability calculations if the dependent variable is, at least, ordinal because the analysis looks at cumulative frequency (which eventually adds up to 100% as one moves along the scores). Data are collected from one group of people (or things). The pattern of the relative number of people (or things) across each score (in each category) on the dependent variable is compared to a predetermined hypothesized pattern. Instead of having to compare each level or category of the dependent variable between the sample and theoretical distributions, the Kolmogorov-Smirnov test uses the efficient strategy of simply identifying the one category that differs the most and testing it to see if it varies more greatly than would be expected by chance.

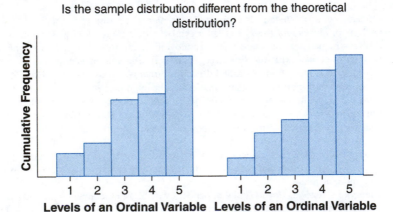

Is the sample distribution different from the theoretical distribution?

Primary Statistical Question

Looking at the level of the dependent variable where the two distributions differ the most, is the difference more than would be expected by chance alone?

Example of a Study That Would Use the Kolmogorov-Smirnov Test

Criminologists in a large city noticed that there seemed to be a changing pattern in the time of day when car thefts were being committed. The old pattern was well established, and a Kolmogorov-Smirnov test was conducted to see if the new pattern really represented a change or was more likely just a temporary chance fluctuation. Records were gathered for 100 recent thefts and compared to the traditional pattern. The data are shown below.

	A.M.						P.M.					
	12–2	2–4	4–6	6–8	8–10	10–12	12–2	2–4	4–6	6–8	8–10	10–12
Old Pattern Cumulative Proportion	.36	.39	.40	.43	.45	.50	.51	.57	.65	.76	.90	1.00
Number of Recent Car Thefts	12	10	2	1	6	10	15	12	15	13	2	2
Cumulative Proportion	.12	.22	.24	.25	.31	.41	.56	.68	.83	.96	.98	1.00

Analysis

The biggest difference between parallel categories, expressed as the difference between the two cumulative proportions, is known as D. It is D that is tested statistically. The biggest difference between observed and expected frequency in this study is in the *midnight to 2 a.m.* category, with a D of .24. In this case, D was found to be significant, which was interpreted to mean that the overall difference in patterns was significant. A fair summary of the difference would be that fewer car thefts now occur late at night than did in the old days.

Things to Consider

- Because it can handle so many levels, this test doesn't require the collapsing of categories into a smaller number, as the **chi-squared** test (see Module 2) sometimes does.
- The Kolmogorov-Smirnov test described here is more formally called the *Kolmogorov-Smirnov one-sample test* to distinguish it from a two-sample version that compares two groups in a manner similar to an **independent *t* test** (see Module 8), but with an ordinal level dependent variable.
- Because the Kolmogorov-Smirnov test works for dependent variables that are ordinal level *and above*, it is sometimes used for interval level dependent variables when one wishes to know if they are distributed in a manner required by a statistical assumption that must be met. For example, it can be used to see if a dependent variable is "normally distributed." The normal curve distribution is precisely defined theoretically, so a sample distribution could be compared to it using the Kolmogorov-Smirnov approach.

Single-Sample *t* Test

Independent Variables	0
Level of Measurement	——
Number of Levels	——
Number of Groups	1
Dependent Variables	**1**
Level of Measurement	Interval
Number of Levels	Many
Measurement Occasions	**1**

Research Design

A single-sample *t* test, as the name suggests, works when you have a single group of people (or things) and you wonder whether they are different in some way from some hypothesized population. The dependent variable here is at the interval level, so the statistical decision is based on whether the sample mean is close enough to the theoretical population's mean that any difference seen in the sample probably occurred by chance.

With single-sample *t* tests, the population that one compares to is almost always theoretical. That is, one isn't usually literally interested in whether a sample was, in fact, drawn from a certain population. The more common research question of interest is whether a sample matches the characteristics that one would expect if that sample wasn't different in some way from this imagined population.

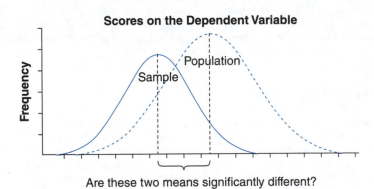

Primary Statistical Question

Could a sample with *this* mean have been randomly drawn from a population with *that* mean?

Example of a Study That Would Use the Single-Sample *t* Test

Flowers produce pollen, a powder that when spread from flower to flower allows for reproduction. A particular type of bean plant relies on bees to visit its flowers, cover themselves with pollen, and fly off and spread the wealth. A botanist knew that one species of this bean plant (*Lathyrus ochroleucus*, if you must know) reproduced very easily compared to other bean plant species and suspected that it was because this species produced more pollen than normal. A single-sample *t* test was conducted to see if this species produced more pollen than other species in the same *genus* (closely related species). The dependent variable was the amount of pollen produced (expressed in number of grains) in a sample of 26 of these particular plants. The sample mean was compared to a known population mean for the genus.

Analysis

The data used, and the results, are shown in this table.

Sample Size	Sample Mean	Sample Standard Deviation	Population Mean	*t*	Significance
26	10,890,000	2,667,000	9,230,000	3.17	*p* = .002

Lathyrus ochroleucus does produce significantly more pollen than your everyday bean plant.

Things to Consider

- The single-sample *t* test is very useful for reporting the results of attitude surveys. Commonly, researchers measure attitude with a series of items that are statements followed by answer options that range from *1* = *strongly disagree* to *5* = *strongly agree*, or something like that. Questions formatted this way are called *Likert-type* items, named after the researcher who first suggested the approach. Because researchers would like to report that attitudes are *positive* or *negative* or that participants *support* or *oppose* a position, a statistical test is needed to show that a sample mean for such items is, in fact, significantly different from a middle or neutral response. A single-sample *t* test can do just that by comparing a sample mean (e.g., 3.2) to a theoretical population mean (e.g., 3.0, which is how a hypothesized population that was neutral would score) and seeing if it's above or below and, therefore, a positive or negative attitude.
- A single-sample *t* test is different from the other procedures grouped into the Frequency Analysis section of this book. Because the dependent variable is interval level, it is actually the mean of the single group that is analyzed, not the frequencies of occurrence of various scores. This test belongs in this section, however, because, like many frequency analysis procedures, there isn't really an independent variable to speak of. One is only interested in whether the single sample of scores likely came from some theoretical population.

Real-Life Study That (Loosely) Inspired This Example

Vonhof, M. J., & Harder, L. D. (1995). Size-number trade-offs and pollen production by papilionaceous legumes. *American Journal of Botany, 82*(2), 230–238.

Fisher Exact Test

Independent Variables	1
Level of Measurement	Nominal
Number of Levels	2
Number of Groups	1
Dependent Variables	1
Level of Measurement	Nominal
Number of Levels	2
Measurement Occasions	1

Research Design

When a researcher is interested in the relationship between two nominal level variables and both of those variables only have two levels, the Fisher exact test is the appropriate statistic to use. Picture a two-by-two table with four squares or *cells*. The two categories on one variable define the two columns and the two categories on the other variable define the two rows. All participants must belong to one and only one cell. If how one scores on one variable makes no difference in how one scores on the other variable, then the frequency of people in each cell of a row should be based only on the overall number of people who happen to be in that category of the related column. Any difference in the expected proportions is tested statistically.

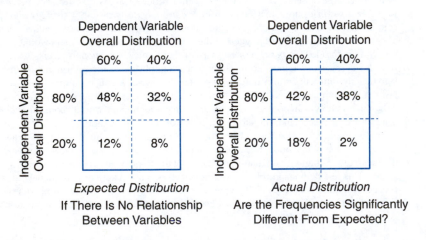

Primary Statistical Question

Do the observed frequencies differ from what one would expect if there were no relationship between the variables?

Example of a Study That Would Use The Fisher Exact Test

In our discussion of the **binomial test** (see Module 1), we learned about the popularity of riddles among Peruvian mountain children. Among other things, that researcher was interested in the relationship between the ability to tell riddles and how children responded when asked questions in class. The nominal independent variable was the ability to tell riddles (*high ability* or *low ability*), and the nominal dependent variable was how students felt when questioned (*anxious* or not *anxious*). Because both variables were nominal with two levels, a Fisher exact test was the right statistic to use.

Analysis

With 30 children in the study, and based on the overall separate distributions of riddling ability and anxiety tendencies found in the sample, a table of expected frequencies could be compared to observed frequencies. The two tables are presented here.

	Expected Frequencies			Actual Frequencies	
	33% Are Anxious	67% Are Not Anxious		33% Are Anxious	67% Are Not Anxious
43% Are Good Riddlers	4 (14%)	9 (29%)	43% Are Good Riddlers	7 (23%)	6 (20%)
57% Are Bad Riddlers	6 (19%)	11 (38%)	57% Are Bad Riddlers	3 (10%)	14 (47%)

The calculations that make up the Fisher exact test found that differences (between the observed values in each cell and the values one would expect if there was no relationship between the two variables) this size *or greater* would only occur 4.5% of the time, $p = .045$. It appears that those who are good at riddles are actually more anxious when questioned in the classroom than those who are less good at riddles.

Things to Consider

- The number of groups for the Fisher exact test is listed here as *1* because the basic research design gathers data from one group of people and then categorizes them into different levels on the nominal independent and dependent variables. It is also reasonable to think of this analysis as involving two groups, however, because the different categories on the independent variable form two independent groups of people. In fact, the independent variable could easily be *experimental or comparison group*, and, then, the design would look very much like traditional group comparison designs.
- Most statistical procedures compute a statistical value (e.g., a correlation, *t*, *F*, or *chi-squared*) that is then compared to some critical value to determine its *p* value or probability. The Fisher exact test is somewhat unusual in that it actually calculates the exact *p* value directly. This is why it is called the Fisher *exact* test.

Real-Life Study That Inspired This Example

Bolton, R. (1977). Riddling and responsibility in highland Peru. *American Ethnologist, 4*(3), 497–516.

Two-Way Chi-Squared

Independent Variables	1
Level of Measurement	Nominal
Number of Levels	2+
Number of Groups	1
Dependent Variables	**1**
Level of Measurement	Nominal
Number of Levels	2+
Measurement Occasions	**1**

Research Design

This chi-squared analysis is perfect when a researcher has two variables at the nominal level, with any number of categories, and wonders if they are related. Data are collected from one group of people and the number of people in each category on each variable is counted and placed in a table. Because this table provides the data that is analyzed, the two-way chi-squared procedure is also called a *contingency table analysis*. The categories on one variable define the columns, and the categories on the other variable define the rows. All participants must belong to one and only one cell. If how one scores on one variable makes no difference in how one scores on the other variable, then the frequency of people in each cell of a row should be based only on the overall number of people who happen to be in that category of the related column. Any difference in the expected proportions is tested statistically.

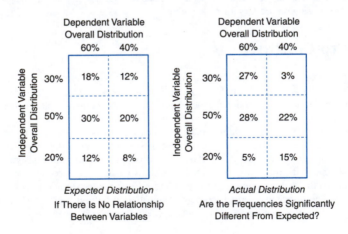

Primary Statistical Question

Does the distribution of people on one variable depend on where they are on the other variable?

Example of a Study That Would Use a Two-Way Chi-Squared Analysis

A researcher at a potato chip company wondered whether customers would prefer their new lemon-flavored chips over their traditional regular potato chips. Having conducted many taste tests like this in the past, though, the researcher also wanted to test a hypothesis about taste tests. Does the order in which you taste something affect your preference? Two nominal level variables were chosen for the study. One variable was potato chip preference (*regular, lemon,* or *no preference*), and the other variable was which one was tasted *last* (half of participants were assigned to each category). One hundred grocery store customers participated in the study. If tasting order made no difference, then the frequency of people preferring regular or lemon (whatever that turned out to be) should be the same regardless of which chip was tasted *last.*

Analysis

The overall preferences were 40% regular, 38% lemon, and 22% no preference. Consumers didn't really like one type of potato chip more than the other. Further, people tended to like whichever potato chip they tasted last. The contingency tables for the study are presented here.

	Expected Frequencies				Actual Frequencies		
	Regular 40	Lemon 38	No Preference 22		Regular 40	Lemon 38	No Preference 22
50 tasted regular last	20	19	11		28	12	10
50 tasted lemon last	20	19	11		12	26	12

The calculated chi-squared, which is based on the differences between expected and actual frequencies, was 11.74. That value was significant at $p = .003$.

Things to Consider

- The two-way chi-squared test is sometimes called *contingency table analysis* because of the layout of the categorical data into rows and columns for analysis. In statistical software (like SPSS*), it is often found as part of a "cross-tabulation" option.
- A **phi correlation coefficient** (see Module 26) indicates the strength of the relationship between two nominal variables. It is often reported as part of a two-way chi-squared analysis.
- Though the two-way chi-squared test works when both variables have exactly two categories, the **Fisher exact test** (see Module 5) is usually more accurate. Specifically, the Fisher exact test works better for sample sizes of 40 or fewer, especially when some cells only contain a few people.
- Like the Fisher exact test, one could think of this analysis as involving more than one group (each level of one variable can be thought of as a group). The two-way chi-squared test, though, is typically framed as looking at the relationship between two variables collected from one sample. The two variables just happen to be at the nominal level.

Real-Life Study That Inspired This Example

Alfaro-Rodriguez, H., Angulo, O., & Mahoney, M. (2007). Be your own placebo: A double paired preference test approach for establishing expected frequencies. *Food Quality and Preference, 18,* 353–361.

SPSS is a registered trademark of International Business Machines Corporation.

PART 2

GROUP COMPARISONS

A popular research strategy is to compare groups of people. The idea is to create groups that represent different levels (or values or scores) of an independent variable. Everyone in the group has the same score on the independent variable. So, if the groups differ on some dependent variable, then that shows there's a relationship between the independent and dependent variable.

A lot of the really famous statistics, like *t* tests and analyses of variance, compare group means to determine significance. Those mean comparison statistics work on the assumption that the dependent variable is at the interval level and, therefore, is normally distributed in the population. That's how they can be so precise and powerful. We don't tend to teach about all the group comparison statistics that work for dependent variables that are not interval level of measurement, however. There are many of those *nonparametric* group comparison statistics that work with nominal and ordinal dependent variables, and they are covered in this section along with those better known mean comparison approaches.

Mann-Whitney Test

Independent Variables	1
Level of Measurement	Nominal
Number of Levels	2
Number of Groups	2
Dependent Variables	1
Level of Measurement	Ordinal
Number of Levels	Many
Measurement Occasions	1

Research Design

The most common design to use a Mann-Whitney test is when exactly two groups of people (or things) are compared on the same ordinal level dependent variable. Groups or categories are used for the comparison, which makes the independent variable nominal. The analysis is based on a rank ordering of all the scores in the analysis from smallest to largest. Then, the assigned *ranks* (i.e., 1, 2, 3, and so on, not the actual scores themselves) in each group are summed and compared.

Primary Statistical Question

Are the summed ranks for each group different from each other?

Example of a Study That Would Use the Mann-Whitney Test

A researcher was interested in a health promotion program for older people offered in senior centers. Programs were offered several times a day, several days a week for many months. In what ways did those who participated frequently differ from those who did not? As the independent variable, two groups of participants were identified—those who came to relatively few sessions (there were 118 of these folks) and those who came to many sessions (there were 29 people in this group). One dependent variable of interest was a common indicator of functional health for this population—the *ability to climb two flights of stairs*. Participants in the study self-reported their stair-climbing ability using a single question with high scores indicating difficulty. The researcher judged that this was an ordinal level variable, so scores were ranked.

Analysis

Imagine that the results of this study looked like this:

Independent Variable	N	Mean Rank	Sum of Ranks
Low attenders	118	78.42	9253.56
High attenders	29	56.03	1624.87

Wilcoxon's W = 1624.87, $p \leq .01$

The researcher concluded that because they had a significantly higher mean rank, low attenders had more trouble climbing stairs. Perhaps their low mobility kept them away from classes.

Things to Consider

- Instead of *Wilcoxon's W* (which is the sum of ranks in the smaller group) it is often a *Mann-Whitney U* and its associated level of significance that is computed. *U* is calculated by first identifying the smallest group (in terms of sample size). For each score in that group, count the number of scores in the *other group* that are smaller. Any scores in the larger group that are equal to the given score in the smaller group are assigned half of a point. There is a count produced for *each score* in that smallest group. *U* is the sum of all those counts.
- If an **independent *t* test** (see Module 8) is being considered, but a researcher isn't sure that the dependent variable should be considered interval level, then the Mann-Whitney test is the best alternative.
- When assigning ranks to scores, there will be lots of ties. If two or more scores are the same, the Mann-Whitney procedure is to assign the *mean* of the ranks they would receive if they were not the same. For example, if ranks 1 through 13 have been assigned and the next two raw scores are both the same, the two available ranks are 14 and 15. The average of those ranks is 14.5. So, 14.5 is assigned as the rank to both those scores and the next score would receive a rank of 16.
- Because three people, Mann, Whitney, and Wilcoxon, all independently suggested this statistical test, the method is probably most fairly called the *Wilcoxon-Mann-Whitney test*. Sometimes the procedure is referred to as the *Wilcoxon rank sum test*.

Real-Life Study That Inspired This Example

Watkins, A. J., & Kligman, E. W. (1993). Attendance patterns of older adults in a health promotion program. *Public Health Reports, 108*(1), 86–90.

Independent *t* Test

Independent Variables	1
Level of Measurement	Nominal
Number of Levels	2
Number of Groups	2
Dependent Variables	1
Level of Measurement	Interval
Number of Levels	Many
Measurement Occasions	1

Research Design

The most common design that uses an independent *t* test is when exactly two different groups of participants (or things) are compared on the same dependent variable. Because groups or categories are used for the comparison, the independent variable is a nominal level variable.

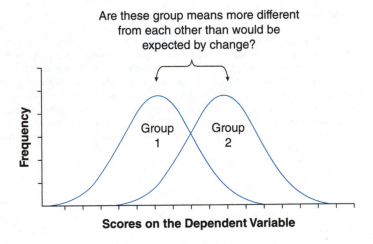

Primary Statistical Question

Are the two groups' means significantly different?

Example of a Study That Would Use an Independent *t* Test

Sixty similar bottles of wine are randomly assigned to one of two groups. One group is stored in a refrigerator for a month; the other group is stored at room temperature for a month. Both groups are then brought to room temperature and tasted by a panel of wine experts. The dependent variable is the rating of taste as assessed by experts on a 1 to 10 scale.

Analysis

Assume the study produced this data necessary for conducting an independent *t* test:

	Sample Size	Mean Rating	Standard Deviation
Group 1: Refrigerated	30	8.03	1.77
Group 2: Room temperature	30	7.07	1.60

Statistical analysis would result in an "observed" *t* value of 2.22, which is associated with a probability of .03. A value of .03 is less than the customary critical *p* value of .05. The difference between the two groups' means is greater than would be expected by chance. The refrigerated bottles of wine tasted better, so it is reasonable to conclude that wine (or, at least, the type of wine used in the study) should be refrigerated.

Things to Consider

- *t* tests are a specific type of **analysis of variance** (see Module 11). So, it is okay to refer to this procedure as analysis of variance. It is analysis of variance with only two groups. If you conduct an analysis of variance using this two-group design, you will get the same result in terms of statistical significance. The analysis of variance's resulting *F* value is the independent *t* test's *t* value squared.
- If you have some concern that the dependent variable is not "really" at the interval or ratio level, consider using nonparametric approaches such as the **two-way chi-squared** (see Module 6) or the **Mann-Whitney test** (see Module 7).
- Statistical comparisons of means often assume that the variability of scores in each group is about the same. Methods exist to judge the equality of the variances (e.g., *Levene's test for homogeneity of variance*). If it is concluded that variances are greatly unequal, there are *t* test procedures that do not require this assumption of equal variance.
- The *p* value reported in the example is two-tailed, which means that a significant difference in either direction would be treated as meaningful. Most researchers are interested in the two-tailed *p* value.
- The term *independent* identifying this type of *t* test refers to the independence of the two groups. Different people (or things) produced the two sets of scores, and they are not associated with each other in any meaningful way. Do not be confused by the fact that we also use the term *independent* to refer to independent variables when discussing research designs.

Median Test

Independent Variables	1
Level of Measurement	Nominal
Number of Levels	2+
Number of Groups	2+
Dependent Variables	1
Level of Measurement	Ordinal
Number of Levels	Many
Measurement Occasions	1

Research Design

The most common design to use a median test is when two or more groups of people (or things) are compared on the same ordinal level dependent variable. Because groups or categories are used for the comparison, the independent variable is a nominal level variable.

Do these groups differ in terms of the frequency
of scores above or below the median?

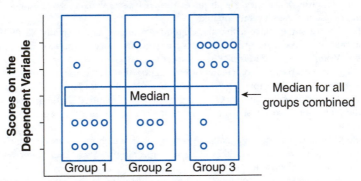

Primary Statistical Question

The median is the score in a group of scores that is the middle point. An equal number of scores are greater than the median as are less than the median. Are the groups' medians significantly different?

Example of a Study That Would Use a Median Test

Ninety-six college students in Australia were asked to respond to attitude questions about what they thought was the cause of the current high unemployment rate. The independent variable was nominal and was the political party to which they belonged (*Conservative, Labor,* or *Liberal*). One specific question was chosen as the dependent variable for the analysis: Do you agree or disagree that the current unemployment rate is due to low motivation of the unemployed? Because it was unclear whether the answer options (*1 = strongly disagree* to *5 = strongly agree*) were truly at the interval level and a single item was used as the dependent variable (which was unlikely to be normally distributed), the researchers decided to treat the dependent variable as ordinal level just to be safe. The hypothesis was that members of the *Conservative Party* would be more likely to view low motivation as one cause of unemployment.

Analysis

The results of median test analyses are presented as the number of people in each group who are *greater than* or *less than* (actually *equal to* or *less than*) the overall median for everyone in the study (think of it as the grand median). If the groups don't differ significantly on the dependent variable, the relative proportion of scores that fall above or below the median should be about the same in every group. Imagine the results looked like this:

	Greater Than the Median	Equal to or Less Than the Median
Conservative	30	6
Labor	17	13
Liberal	18	12

Note: The overall median for all groups combined was 3.

Assuming the results were statistically significant (and for this data, the *p* value was .04), one can conclude that *Conservative Party* members are more likely to consider low motivation as one factor influencing the unemployment rate.

Things to Consider

- Because the median test compares the frequency of scores in different categories (above or below the median), the underlying mathematics is the same as is used for a **chi-squared** analysis.
- Statistics books sometimes describe the median test as appropriate only when there are exactly two groups, but it can just as easily be used when there are more than two groups. In fact, when there are only two groups, the **Mann-Whitney test** is probably a better choice than the median test because it is more accurate.
- The median test is so named, obviously, because it tests whether several medians are different from each other. By the same logic, statisticians might have chosen to call the *t* **test** or **analysis of variance** the *mean test*.

Real-Life Study That Inspired This Example

Feather, N. T. (1985). Attitudes, values, and attributions: Explanations of unemployment. *Journal of Personality and Social Psychology, 48*(4), 876–889.

Kruskal-Wallis Test

Independent Variables	1
Level of Measurement	Nominal
Number of Levels	2+
Number of Groups	2+
Dependent Variables	1
Level of Measurement	Ordinal
Number of Levels	Many
Measurement Occasions	1

Research Design

The Kruskal-Wallis test works when two or more groups of people (or things) are compared on the same ordinal level dependent variable. Because groups or categories are used for the comparison, the independent variable is a nominal level variable. The strategy is to assign ranks to all the scores on the dependent variable by putting them in order and then place those ranks into the different groups or categories defined by the independent variable. The total ranks in each group are compared statistically.

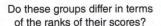

Do these groups differ in terms of the ranks of their scores?

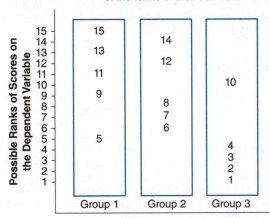

Primary Statistical Question

Do the groups differ in terms of their summed rank scores?

Example of a Study That Would Use the Kruskal-Wallis Test

In our discussion of the **Mann-Whitney test** (see Module 7), we described a study about a health promotion program for older people offered in a variety of senior centers. A different research question in that study involved a nominal independent variable with four categories and a dependent variable at the ordinal level, so a Kruskal-Wallis analysis was conducted. The independent variable was *participation level*, which was divided into four levels (*low attendance*, *some attendance*, *good attendance*, and *high attendance*). The dependent variable was an index of *social isolation*, the total score of eight items that asked about loneliness, interactions with society, and so on. The study involved 176 people.

Analysis

Most of the values used in the analysis cannot be shown here, but all 176 scores on the social isolation index were ranked, 1 through 176, and the ranks were grouped by the four attendance categories. The total rankings in the four groups were analyzed using Kruskal-Wallis's equations. The resulting value, a "KW," was 9.78, which was significant at $p \leq .01$ for this sample size. Those who attended less had higher scores on the social isolation index.

Things to Consider

- The Kruskal-Wallis *KW* is sometimes reported as a chi-squared because researchers are more familiar with that. They are different values, though, and have different associated probabilities. The Kruskal-Wallis analysis provides for easy conversion to an equivalent chi-squared value. Before computer software, it was easier to look up critical values for the chi-squared test than for a Kruskal-Wallis analysis of variance, so this conversion has become common.
- Notice in the example study that if the independent variable is actually higher than nominal level, it is ordinal. If the researcher framed the analysis as the correlational relationship between attendance and social isolation instead of differences between groups, then a **Spearman correlation coefficient** (see Module 25) would have been the "right" statistic to use.
- The Kruskal-Wallis approach is a great alternative to **analysis of variance** (see Module 11) when you are not 100% sure that your dependent variable is at the interval level or is normally distributed in the population.
- The research design for the Kruskal-Wallis test is the same as the design for which the **median test** (see Module 9) is appropriate. The median test, however, does not make use of all the rank order information available in the data as the analysis is based only on whether each score is above or below the overall median. If your ordinal variable can be meaningfully ordered all along its range, the Kruskal-Wallis is best to use because it uses all the ranking information. Statisticians refer to statistics that take more information into account as more *powerful*, and the Kruskal-Wallis is more powerful than the median test.

Real-Life Study That Inspired This Example

Watkins, A. J., & Kligman, E. W. (1993). Attendance patterns of older adults in a health promotion program. *Public Health Reports, 108*, 86–90.

Analysis of Variance

Independent Variables	1
Level of Measurement	Nominal
Number of Levels	2+
Number of Groups	2+
Dependent Variables	1
Level of Measurement	Interval
Number of Levels	Many
Measurement Occasions	1

Research Design

An analysis of variance is used when groups of people (or things) are compared on the same dependent variable. The nominal independent variable can have any number of levels, so more than two groups can be compared at the same time. Because the dependent variable is at the interval level, the means of each group of scores are used for the statistical analysis. This sort of design is very common in experimental studies where people in different groups receive different treatments, drugs, or interventions and one wishes to compare them. It is also used when people are already in different groups naturally or in some way that the researcher did not assign.

Are these group means more different
from each other than would be
expected by chance?

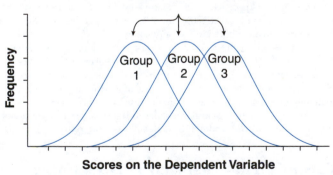

Scores on the Dependent Variable

Primary Statistical Question

Are the groups' means significantly different?

Example of a Study That Would Use an Analysis of Variance

An educational researcher wondered which of three math teaching methods worked best. Fifty-three fourth graders were randomly assigned to one of three classrooms for a weeklong training in solving word problems. The nominal independent variable was the three teaching methods—using the textbook only, using traditional teaching methods, and using a new method that involved following a standardized set of steps to solve the problem. The interval level dependent variable was performance on a ten-question math test (with possible scores from 0 to 10).

Analysis

The data was analyzed using analysis of variance, which compares the differences between the three mean scores on the math test to differences that would be expected by chance alone.

	Sample Size	Mean	Standard Deviation
Book only	19	7.53	.51
Traditional method	19	7.79	.85
New method	15	8.20	.56

The resulting F with this data was 4.28, which was significant, $p = .02$. Follow-up independent t tests found that the only significant difference was between the new method and *book only*.

Things to Consider

- When one has exactly two groups to compare, either analysis of variance or an **independent t test** (see Module 8) may be used. Both will provide the same result in terms of statistical significance. In fact, the t one would get from the independent t test is the square root of the F one would get from the analysis of variance.
- Because an analysis of variance only tells us if there is some difference among the groups, follow-up analyses are often done to see where the differences are. These follow-up tests are called *post hoc* (Latin for "after this") analyses and are a series of independent t tests for pairs of means taken two at a time. If there are many post hoc comparisons to do and the researcher is worried that some comparisons will be significant just by chance, a critical level of significance lower than .05 is often chosen.
- Mathematically, analysis of variance will work with any number of groups. Practically speaking, however, most designs have just a few groups to compare. This is because most research questions are only interested in comparing a few groups and, also, because real-life studies often can't produce large enough sample sizes in each group to perform a meaningful analysis.
- The common abbreviation for analysis of variance is ANOVA. This is a strange abbreviation (it should be *AoV*, and it is, also oddly, in all upper case letters. The reason is that ANOVA originated as the computer programming name for the procedure that ran the analysis in the old-timey days of mainframe computers. This is also why **analysis of covariance** (see Module 13) is abbreviated ANCOVA and **multivariate analysis of variance** (see Module 14) is shortened to MANOVA.

Real-Life Study That Inspired This Example

Hohn, R. L., & Frey, B. (2002). Heuristic training and performance in elementary mathematical problem solving. *Journal of Educational Research, 95*(6), 374–380.

Two-Way Analysis of Variance

Independent Variables	2
Level of Measurement	Nominal
Number of Levels	2+
Number of Groups	2+
Dependent Variables	1
Level of Measurement	Interval
Number of Levels	Many
Measurement Occasions	1

Research Design

A two-way analysis of variance is used when groups of people (or things) are compared on the same interval level dependent variable. It differs from a regular analysis of variance because there are two independent variables, not just one. *Two-way* refers to the two independent variables. In addition to seeing if the dependent variable differs for either of the independent variables, a two-way analysis of variance also looks to see if the relationship between one independent variable and the outcome depends on which level you're at on the other independent variable. This phenomenon, where the effect of one independent variable depends on the other independent variable, is called an *interaction*. Interactions may be best understood visually. If you plot the mean scores on the dependent variable for each group and connect the dots, you get two lines showing the effect of each independent variable. If the lines are not parallel, there is an interaction.

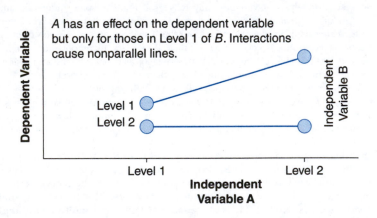

Primary Statistical Questions

1. Are the groups' means significantly different for either independent variable?

2. Is the effect of one independent variable on the dependent variable different based on which group one is in on the other independent variable?

Example of a Study That Would Use Two-Way Analysis of Variance

A large waist circumference (how big around we are) is a risk factor for chronic disease and other health problems. Researchers knew that among children aged 5 to 12 there is a small sex difference in roundness and also a small relationship with age. Older children and girls, in general, tend to have slightly larger waists. These differences, by themselves, aren't usually big enough to be very interesting. They wondered, though, if there was an interaction between the two. In other words, does the sex difference vary depending on age? Or, to say it the opposite way, is the relationship between age and waist size different for boys than for girls? To find out, they gathered data and measured the waists of 179 children.

Analysis

Some of the data used for the two-way analysis of variance and a chart of the means are shown here. Two age groups were used as one independent variable (ages 5–8, ages 9–12) and sex was the other. Waist circumference measured in centimeters was the dependent variable.

	Waist Circumference	
	Mean	**Standard Deviation**
Boys Young	63.08	5.50
Old	64.10	5.58
Girls Young	64.06	7.20
Old	64.41	8.07

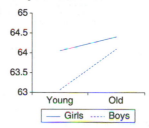

Part of the two-way analysis of variance tests whether any interaction is statistically significant. For this analysis, there was a significant interaction ($F = 5.22$, $p = .03$). The sex difference is greater at a younger age but tends to disappear as children get older. That's why analyses that only take one of the independent variables into account do not often find significant results.

Things to Consider

- One need not be looking for an interaction to use two-way analysis of variance. It is efficient to use any time there are two nominal level independent variables of interest.
- A regular analysis of variance is sometimes called a one-way analysis of variance because it uses only one independent variable.
- Mathematically, we can use as many nominal independent variables as we want and do three-way analyses of variance or four-way or more. It becomes difficult to conduct and interpret these analyses, however, with greater than three independent variables. Even talking about just three independent variables is tough.
- The statistical term *interaction* means the same thing as when we talk about *drug interactions*. There is a drug interaction when one drug affects you differently depending on how much of the other drug is in your system.

Real-Life Study That Inspired This Example

Ghosh, A., Chatterjee, D., Bandyopadhyay, A. R., & Chaudhuri, A. B. D. (2006). Age and sex variation of body mass index and waist circumference among the Santal children of Tharkhand, India. *Anthropologischer Anzeiger, 64*(1), 83–89.

Analysis of Covariance

Independent Variables	1
Level of Measurement	Nominal
Number of Levels	2+
Number of Groups	2+
Dependent Variables	**1**
Level of Measurement	Interval
Number of Levels	Many
Covariate Variables	**1**
Level of Measurement	Interval
Number of Levels	Many
Measurement Occasions	**1**

Research Design

Analysis of covariance is unique in this book because the research design involves a third type of variable that is neither an independent nor a dependent variable. The category of *covariate* has been added to the summary table that begins this section. A covariate is a variable that the researcher believes is related to the dependent variable, but the researcher wishes to control for it. Controlling for a variable statistically means to adjust the results to what they would be if all participants were equal on that variable. Analysis-of-covariance designs are similar to **analysis of variance** (see Module 11) designs in that they have one nominal level independent variable and one interval level dependent variable. Additionally, there is one interval level covariate. The analysis uses correlational information between the covariate and the dependent variable to predict what the dependent variable scores would be based only on the covariate and calculate those predicted group means. Any difference that remains is assumed to be due to the independent variable, and one conducts a regular analysis of variance on those new "adjusted" group means.

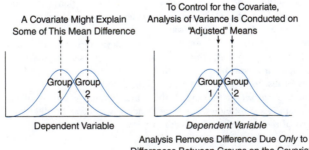

Primary Statistical Question

Are the adjusted groups' means significantly different from each other?

Example of a Study That Would Use an Analysis of Covariance

Males and females with thyroid disease may differ in terms of how the disease affects their eyes. Many thyroid patients have a bulging of the eyes called Graves' disease. A physician designed a study with sex (male or female) as the nominal independent variable and an index of the severity of Graves' disease as the interval level dependent variable. In the study were 101 thyroid patients with the eye disease, and an initial analysis did find a difference, with males scoring higher on the eye disease index ($F = 11.76$, $p < .001$). The researcher noticed that the males in the study were older than the females (53.8 years compared to 48.2 years) and was worried that age might be an alternative explanation for the group differences. Older people in general might have worse symptoms. So, an analysis of covariance was conducted controlling for age, an interval level variable, by using it as the covariate.

Analysis

The correlation between age and the eye disease index turned out to be .37 ($p < .01$), so it was a good candidate as a covariate. This correlation was used to adjust the means to what they would be if age did not play any role in the group differences. The initial analysis of variance data is shown, along with the adjusted means used in the analysis of covariance.

Independent Variable	Sample Size	Eye Disease Index		
		Mean	Standard Deviation	Adjusted Means
Females	81	.89	.22	.85
Males	20	.70	.22	.71

The analysis of covariance that compared the adjusted means also resulted in a significant F (7.34, $p < .01$). Even controlling for age, males tend to have more severe Graves' disease symptoms.

Things to Consider

- Because one believes that covariates affect the dependent variable, it is reasonable to label covariates as independent variables. Some textbooks and websites do this. You can think of covariates as independent variables you want to remove from your analysis and rule out as possible explanations for your results.
- There is no reason to conduct an analysis of covariance if the covariate is not related to the dependent variable or the independent variable groups do not differ on the covariate.
- A strong group design eliminates the necessity of controlling for covariates. By randomly assigning participants to the levels of the independent variable (the different groups), all potential covariates are likely equalized among groups. At least, that's the assumption.

Real-Life Study That Inspired This Example

Perros, P., Crombie, A. L., Matthews, J. N. S., & Kendall-Taylor, P. (1993). Age and gender influence the severity of thyroid-associated ophthalmopathy: A study of 101 patients attending a combined thyroid-eye clinic. *Clinical Endocrinology, 38*(4), 367–372.

Multivariate Analysis of Variance

Independent Variables	1
Level of Measurement	Nominal
Number of Levels	2+
Number of Groups	2+
Dependent Variables	**2+**
Level of Measurement	Interval
Number of Levels	Many
Measurement Occasions	**1**

Research Design

A multivariate analysis of variance is used when groups of people (or things) are compared on more than one interval level dependent variable. The analytic procedure does several statistical tests at once. First, it sees whether an analysis of variance for any of the dependent variables would be significant and shows the results for all of those analyses of variance. Second, it also tells us whether any *linear composite* of the dependent variables differ significantly among groups. Because the dependent variables might be correlated and have some unmeasured variable in common, that "latent" (hidden) variable is also compared between groups.

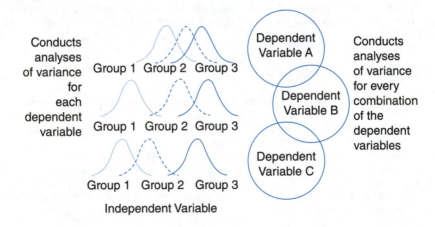

Primary Statistical Questions

1. Are the groups' means significantly different for any of the dependent variables?

2. Do the groups differ on any combination of the dependent variables?

Example of a Study That Would Use an Analysis of Variance

Grandparents and parents often have different perspectives on the proper family role of grandparents. This may be particularly true in African American families where grandparents traditionally play important roles. About 200 black grandparents and 125 black parents (unrelated to each other) were surveyed to see if there were differences on three issues: *satisfaction* (are grandparents satisfied with their role in the family?), *frustration* (do grandparents get frustrated with their grandchildren?), and *teaching* (do grandparents teach grandchildren what they should?). This study had one independent variable (*generation*), which was nominal (*grandparents* and *parents*), and three interval level dependent variables.

Analysis

Scores on the three dependent variables by the two groups are shown (SD = standard deviation):

	Satisfaction		Frustration		Teaching	
	Mean	SD	Mean	SD	Mean	SD
Parents	3.43	.44	3.34	.61	3.48	.60
Grandparents	3.24	.47	3.21	.62	3.57	.53

Taking into account some data not shown here, such as correlations among the dependent variables, the multivariate F was 6.57, which was significant at the .001 level. This suggested that there were differences to be found somewhere among the dependent variables. Follow-up analyses of variance found that grandparents were less satisfied with their role than parents knew ($F = 7.42$, $p \leq .001$) but also less frustrated with their grandchildren than parents assumed ($F = 4.23$, $p \leq .001$). There was no significant disagreement on whether grandparents teach grandchildren what they should ($F = 1.89$, $p \leq .17$).

Things to Consider

- A multivariate analysis of variance performs several **analyses of variance** at the same time (see Module 11). This is comparable to the way that an analysis of variance performs several **independent t tests** at the same time (see Module 8).
- This complex idea of using the shared overlap among variables as a variable of its own is also used in **canonical correlation** (see Module 34) where the linear composites of multiple predictor variables and multiple criterion variables might be related to each other.
- A multivariate analysis of variance has a long sequence of follow-up tests. If the multivariate analysis of variance F is significant, then follow-up analyses of variance are conducted to see which (if any) dependent variables differ across groups. For any of those analyses of variance that have significant Fs, follow-up independent t tests are conducted to locate the specific significant differences between groups.
- There is little value in conducting a multivariate analysis of variance if the dependent variables are unrelated and conceptually distinct. One might as well conduct a series of separate analyses of variance because they are simpler to interpret.

Real-Life Study That Inspired This Example

Strom, R., Strom, S., Collinsworth, P., Strom, P., & Griswold, D. (1996). Intergenerational relationships in black families. *International Journal of Sociology of the Family, 26*(2), 129–141.

PART 3

REPEATED MEASURES ANALYSES

R epeated measures analyses involve comparing the scores for people (or things) who have been measured on the same variable more than one time. This section includes procedures for determining significant differences or changes among repeated sets of scores for dependent variables that are at the nominal, ordinal, or interval level of measurement.

There are three situations where repeated measures analyses are used:

1. People are measured on a dependent variable. Time passes, or we do something to them, and then they are measured again on the same dependent variable using the same exact test or instrument. Sometimes they are measured more than twice. Researchers are interested in whether scores have changed between measurement occasions. This is a "pretest posttest" design.

2. People are measured on a dependent variable while in, or having just been in, some condition or context. Then, they are placed in a different condition and are measured again on the same dependent variable using the same exact test or instrument. Sometimes they are measured in more than two conditions. Any differences are seen not as change over time but as the different conditions having different effects on the dependent variable.

3. The same measure or group of items is used to measure different dependent variables in the same group of people. For example, an attitude scale might ask the same sample of customers about their attitude toward a restaurant's service and the restaurant's food. The two sets of responses can be compared to see which is more positive.

All of these designs are considered repeated measures analyses, and the same statistical analytical strategy is used for all three. The right strategy is determined by the level of measurement of the independent and dependent variables and the number of sets of scores (which is the number of measurement occasions).

McNemar Change Test

Independent Variables	1
Level of Measurement	Nominal
Number of Levels	2
Number of Groups	1
Dependent Variables	1
Level of Measurement	Nominal
Number of Levels	2+
Measurement Occasions	2

Research Design

		After	
		Category 1	Category 2
Before	Category 1	16	12
Before	Category 2	4	8

		After	
		Category 1	Category 2
Before	Category 1		These people have changed.
Before	Category 2	These people have changed.	

People Who Have Changed Categories

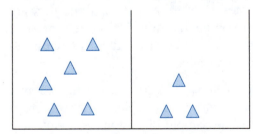

Started in Category 1 but have now changed to a different category

Started in Category 2 but have now changed to a different category

Is the number from each beginning category who have now changed categories equal?

With this design, people (or things) begin in one category, and after some intervention by the independent variable, they may have moved to another category. One group of people is used and measured twice.

Primary Statistical Question

Is the distribution of *those who changed* equal across starting categories?

Example of a Study That Would Use the McNemar Change Test

Researchers believed that beginning social service professionals making incorrect judgments about clients would change their mind after discussions involving other social service professionals. A videotape of a 90-year-old woman being interviewed by a nurse was shown to 421 participants. The "right" judgment to make was defined as the judgment made by experienced professionals consulted by the researchers. After forming an initial judgment about whether the woman needed services, there was a period of collaborative discussion about the woman. Afterward, some participants changed their judgment. The number of people who changed their judgment was counted and further broken down into two categories, those who changed their minds from the right judgment to the wrong judgment and those who changed their mind from the wrong judgment to the right one. It was hypothesized that if the professionals changed their minds after the discussion, more of them would change their judgment from wrong to right than the other way around. The independent variable for the study was *taking part in the collaborative discussion* and the dependent variable was the direction of the change (*right to wrong* or *wrong to right*).

Analysis

The McNemar change test uses a **chi-squared** (see Module 2) analysis using only those who changed their minds. In this study, let's say that out of the 421 people, 308 changed their judgments: 280 went from wrong to right and 28 went from right to wrong.

If the independent variable (the discussions) did not have any effect, then any changes in judgment would be equally as likely to have been from *wrong to right* as from *right to wrong*. In other words, the expected number in each category is an equal number. In this case, that expected frequency is $308 \div 2 = 154$.

The chi-squared test comparing 280 to 154 (or 28 to 154) resulted in a large chi-squared value that is significant at the $p \leq .001$ level.

Collaborative discussion with other professionals greatly improved the quality of judgments.

Things to Consider

- McNemar is pronounced MAC-neh-marr.
- Because a chi-squared test is the underlying analysis for the McNemar change test, the number of categories (i.e., the number of levels of the dependent variable) may be greater than two, and there may be many possible combinations of changes (from any of several categories to any of several categories).

Real-Life Study That Inspired This Example

Read, M., & Gear, T. (2007). Developing professional judgment with the aid of a "low profile" group support system. *The Journal of the Operational Research Society, 58*(8), 1021–1029.

Wilcoxon Signed Ranks Test

Independent Variables	1
Level of Measurement	Nominal
Number of Levels	2
Number of Groups	1
Dependent Variables	1
Level of Measurement	Ordinal
Number of Levels	2
Measurement Occasions	2

Research Design

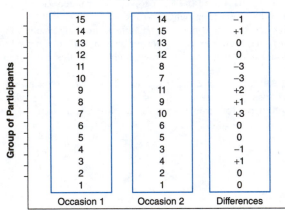

Rank Order on the Dependent Variable

Occasion 1	Occasion 2	Differences
15	14	−1
14	15	+1
13	13	0
12	12	0
11	8	−3
10	7	−3
9	11	+2
8	9	+1
7	10	+3
6	6	0
5	5	0
4	3	−1
3	4	+1
2	2	0
1	1	0

Do the two measurement occasions differ
in terms of the ranks of their scores?

This statistical test is designed for situations where one group of people (or things) has been measured exactly twice. Whatever happens between the two measurement occasions (or however the two conditions differ) is the nominal level independent variable in this design, and the dependent variable is at the ordinal level. Because the dependent variable is represented by a set of scores in some rank order, raw scores can be turned into their ranks (within each measurement occasion) and then compared across the two measurement times. The calculations involve subtracting the ranks on the first occasion from the ranks on the second occasion.

Some pairs of ranks will differ from each other, resulting in either negative or positive values. All of those values are then, themselves, ranked from smallest to largest. Multiplying those values by their new ranks results in a statistic called *W*, where bigger is better, and known statistical probabilities allow for a level of significance to be attached to each *W*.

Primary Statistical Question

Are the rank orders for participants the same on both occasions?

Example of a Study That Would Use the Wilcoxon Signed Ranks Test

Researchers were curious about how much people would cooperate with other players in a game that required working toward a common goal to win the game and win a little money. If the rules of the game allowed players to "punish" each other, would they participate more and contribute more in terms of working toward the common goal? The researcher used 14 participants and had them play the game twice; one time allowed punishment of other players and the other time did not. In this study the independent variable was nominal (which *condition* or set of game rules was used), and the dependent variable was at least ordinal (how much each player participated measured using a scoring system that gave more points for greater participation).

Analysis

The raw participation scores for each participant were ranked after playing the game under the *no-punishment* option condition. They were then ranked again after the second game that used the *punishment-allowed* condition. The rankings were matched up and one set of ranks was subtracted from the other. Application of the Wilcoxon signed ranks test produced a W of 21. A W that large or larger with a sample size of 14 possible ranks would occur with random data less than 5% of the time, so the comparison was statistically significant ($W = 21$, $p = .04$).

The direction of the mean rank difference led to an interpretation that more cooperation occurred when punishment was allowed.

Things to Consider

- It's worth emphasizing with this test and all tests designed for ordinal level scores on the dependent variable that *the original raw scores are not rankings*. People weren't asked to place things in a rank order, for example. Their scores are placed in order after the fact by the researcher and the ranks are assigned at that time.
- As with all repeated measures, the Wilcoxon signed ranks test can be used any time two sets of scores can be associated with each other. There are some common designs using this test that compare two sets of scores from different people who have been matched up in some reasonable way (e.g., they are at the same ability level, they are siblings, they are partners, and so on).
- Some statistical books and software compute a value called T instead of W for their Wilcoxon signed ranks analyses. Consequently, you sometimes see this called a Wilcoxon T test. This can lead to some confusion with the t test. The research design is the same as for a paired samples t test, but with a t test, the dependent variable is at the interval level.
- It is the presence of a negative or positive sign for each difference between pairs of ranks and the name of its developer, Frank Wilcoxon (1892–1965), that gives this test its name.

Real-Life Study That Inspired This Example

Fehr, E., & Gachter, S. (2002). Altruistic punishment in humans. *Nature, 415*, 137–140.

Paired-Samples *t* Test

Independent Variables	1
Level of Measurement	Nominal
Number of Levels	2
Number of Groups	1
Dependent Variables	1
Level of Measurement	Interval
Number of Levels	Many
Measurement Occasions	2

Research Design

The most common design to use a paired samples *t* test has one group measured twice on the same dependent variable. The dependent variable is interval level and the independent variable is whatever happens to the group between the two measurement times. There are two groups (or samples) of scores produced by one group of people (or things).

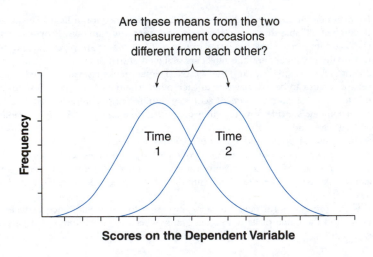

Are these means from the two measurement occasions different from each other?

Frequency

Time 1   Time 2

Scores on the Dependent Variable

Primary Statistical Question

Are the means from the two measurement occasions significantly different from each other?

Example of a Study That Would Use a Paired-Samples *t* Test

A school district instituted an incentive system for teachers that paid salary bonuses for high attendance. The independent variable was the presence of the incentive policy. The dependent variable was the number of days absent for the academic year, an interval level variable (actually, ratio level). Absences were measured twice, the year before the policy and at the end of the first year of the policy. Research participants were 292 teachers.

Analysis

As with all *t* tests, means and standard deviations provide the data.

Measurement Occasion	Mean	SD	Mean Difference	*t*	*p*
Last year	7.21	4.0	1.87	6.18	$p \leq .001$
This year	5.34	3.3			

There was a significant decrease in absences per year under the new system.

Things to Consider

- It is actually the difference between the two means that is tested. That mean difference is treated as a single-sample mean and compared to 0 using a **single-sample *t* test** (see Module 4).
- The design for the paired-samples *t* test shown here is how it is usually presented in textbooks, with a single group measured twice on the exact same measure. A paired-samples *t* test, though, is appropriate any time there are two sets of scores that are likely related and one wishes to know if the means of those two sets of scores are different. So, one could use two groups measured on the same instrument on just one occasion, if the two groups' scores might be related and could be paired up (e.g., pairs of spouses are asked their political views). One could also use a paired-samples *t* test with one group, measured once, on two different measures that are believed to be related (e.g., two attitude instruments using the same items to ask about similar things). For this to work, though, the two measures must be on the "same scale" with the same possible scores, the same range and variability, and so on.
- Any time two sets of scores can be paired up and are correlated, the paired-samples *t* test is more powerful than the **independent *t* test** (see Module 8). The key is there must be a reasonable way to partner up the pairs of scores.
- Output from statistical software sometimes includes the correlation between the matched sets of scores. Do not mistake the *p* value associated with that correlation as the significance of the *t* test itself. The correlation is shown because there is a simple formula for calculating *t* that uses it.
- The paired-samples *t* test is sometimes referred to as the *dependent* t test.
- The *paired-samples* t test is labeled in many places as the *paired-sample* t test (with *sample* being singular). This seems wrong grammatically.

Real-Life Study That Inspired This Example

Jacobson, S. L. (1989). The effects of pay incentives on teacher absenteeism. *The Journal of Human Resources, 24*(2), 280–286.

Cochran Q Test

Independent Variables	1
Level of Measurement	Nominal
Number of Levels	2+
Number of Groups	1
Dependent Variables	**1**
Level of Measurement	Nominal
Number of Levels	2+
Measurement Occasions	**2+**

Research Design

With this design, people (or things) are in one category on one occasion or under one condition and on other measurement occasions they may be in different categories. Typical designs assess participants, and then after some intervention by the independent variable they are assessed again and then again on a third occasion. Or the same group of people may be assessed on three different measures that produce scores all on the same scale to see if categorization differs (e.g., three different judges or three different placement tests). The key is that one uses the Cochran Q test whenever the dependent variable is *nominal* (*at least* nominal) and there are more than two measurement occasions.

The statistical analysis looks only at whether the scores are consistent across each level of the independent variable and is not interested in the actual scores themselves. Data are lined up in a table, and the mathematics involve calculating what the total of the scores would be across all levels of the independent variable if there was perfect consistency and comparing that value with the actual total of scores across categories. A value, Q, is produced, and a larger Q is more significant than a smaller one and indicates that scores are related to the independent variable.

	Three Different Conditions		
Participant	**Level 1**	**Level 2**	**Level 3**
1	1	1	1
2	1	1	2
3	2	2	2
4	2	2	1
5	1	1	1
6	2	2	2
7	2	2	2

Note: 1 and *2* represent two possible nominal scores on a dependent variable.

Primary Statistical Question

Do participants get the same score on the dependent variable for every condition of the independent variable?

Example of a Study That Would Use the Cochran Q Test

A snake expert wondered whether the normally aggressive cottonmouth snake would react less defensively if it got used to being handled. The expert designed a study where 13 different cottonmouth snakes were picked up and their reactions were observed and scored on a 5-point scale based on how much different body parts (e.g., tail, head, tongue) moved. Then, after being handled daily for three days, the defensive reactions were measured again. Finally, after two more days of being handled frequently, the snakes were assessed on their defensiveness one more time.

The independent variable in this study was *being picked up frequently* and was measured as a nominal variable with three levels (Day 1, Day 3, Day 5). The dependent variable was the observational rating about the number and type of body movements and was treated as ordinal.

Analysis

Data for the Cochran Q test were collected for each snake and analyzed in terms of whether the scores were the same on Day 1, Day 3, and Day 5. The equations for calculating Q were applied, and the results were statistically significant ($Q = 5.0$, $p = .03$). This indicated that the snakes' behavior did change over time.

To identify the direction of the change and interpret results, the mean behavior scores were examined. On Day 1, the mean level of behavior was 4.1 (on the 5-point scale used to measure the dependent variable), on Day 3 it was 3.0, and by Day 5 it had dropped to 2.5. Handling snakes does make them less aggressive.

Things to Consider

- The group of participants compared across conditions need not be literally the same people (though that is the most common design for the Cochran Q test). Groups of people that have been matched up on some important control variable can be used and treated as if they are the same people for purposes of the analysis. All that's necessary is that sets of participants' scores can be lined up into columns side by side in a way that makes sense.
- The Cochran Q test is an extension of the **McNemar change test** (see Module 15) in the same way that **repeated measures analysis of variance** (see Module 20) is an extension of the **paired-samples t test** (see Module 17).
- Cochran's Q is useful when you are not positive that your dependent variable is truly at the interval level. One can assume it is at least ordinal and safely use a Q test. Like most statistical analyses that are *nonparametric* (designed for dependent variables that are not normally distributed), however, Cochran's Q is less powerful and makes use of less information than analyses that use interval level variables. In other words, use interval level variables whenever possible and reasonable.
- With more than just a few participants or with many levels of the dependent variable, the **two-way chi-squared** analysis (see Module 6) works perfectly well. It is just as accurate and might be more familiar to researchers than the Cochran Q test.

Real-Life Study That Inspired This Example

Glaudas, X. (2004). Do cottonmouths (Agkistrodon piscivorus) habituate to human confrontations? *Southeastern Naturalist, 3*(1), 129–138.

Friedman Test

Independent Variables	1
Level of Measurement	Nominal
Number of Levels	2+
Number of Groups	1
Dependent Variables	**1**
Level of Measurement	Ordinal
Number of Levels	2+
Measurement Occasions	**2+**

Research Design

The Friedman test compares individual scores across time or across multiple conditions. The independent variable is nominal and the dependent variable must be at least ordinal. Because the dependent scores are ordinal, they can be turned into ranks for analysis. The strategy is to rank order all the scores for each person individually *across conditions*. So, if there are three conditions, each person's raw score becomes a 1, 2, or 3 for each of those conditions. If the raw score is the same for an individual in two different conditions, the average of the two possible ranks is used. Then, the ranks in each condition are summed (or averaged) and compared. If the independent variable has no relationship with, or an effect on, the dependent variable, then the totals of the ranks in each condition should be almost equal.

Raw Scores			
Participants	Time 1	Time 2	Time 3
1	12	10	9
2	16	15	15
3	15	12	8
4	11	13	10

Ranked Scores			
Participants	Time 1	Time 2	Time 3
1	1	2	3
2	1	2.5	2.5
3	1	2	3
4	2	1	3
Total Ranks	**5**	**7.5**	**11.5**
Are these total ranks equal?			

A value is computed from these data with a known set of probabilities, and if it is significant, one concludes that the ranked scores are not the same across conditions. Following a significant result, there is a fairly simple formula to determine the size in difference between any pair of summed ranks. This way one can find out where the differences lie.

Primary Statistical Question

Do participants get the same ranked score on the dependent variable for every condition of the independent variable?

Example of a Study That Would Use the Friedman Test

People who frequently and involuntarily repeat sounds, especially when starting to speak words that begin with consonants, are described as having a *stutter*. Researchers wondered whether those who stutter could improve their ability to quickly start and stop a single sound, such as "ah." A study was designed where a group of 10 young adults who stutter practiced in a laboratory setting to quickly say "ah" whenever they heard a signal tone. They were measured on three occasions to see if they would decrease how long it took to complete the sound. The independent variable for this study was *practice* measured at the nominal level (the three sessions). The dependent variable (*utterance speed*) was treated as at least ordinal level (and not interval because of some technical concerns).

Analysis

The actual raw data used is not shown here, but imagine it placed in a table with ten rows (one for each person) and three columns for scores in each of the three sessions. Each person's three scores were ranked across the three sessions. As a summary, the median scores are shown here, though the ranks for each person are actually used in the calculations.

Session 1	Session 2	Session 3
.67 seconds	.61 seconds	.57 seconds

Taking into account the sample size (n = 10) and the actual rankings across conditions, a Friedman analysis found a significant difference ($p \leq .01$). This suggests that those who stutter have some control over the speed with which they make individual sounds.

Things to Consider

- The Friedman test is similar to the **Wilcoxon signed ranks test** (see Module 16), which also makes use of a repeatedly measured ordinal level dependent variable, but it can be used for many different conditions or measurement occasions. The Wilcoxon, which specializes in comparison between exactly two conditions, can be used for follow-up analyses after a significant Friedman result.
- A variety of "corrections," or specialized equations, are used for certain situations in computing the statistical value, called an F_r, used in the Friedman test. For example, if there were ties in the ranked data, a different F_r equation is used to account for that. Likewise, if there are many conditions or many participants, the F_r is treated as a chi-squared and the known probabilities of a chi-squared are used to determine statistical significance.
- As with all repeated measures analyses, and shown in the example study used here, the Friedman test does not require that the comparisons across conditions actually be the same group of participants. There only needs to be a way to match up scores across occasions. So matched subjects who are actually different people but share something important in common can be used.

Real-Life Study That Inspired This Example

Adams, M. R., & Hayden, P. (1976). The ability of stutterers and non-stutterers to initiate and terminate phonation during production of an isolated vowel. *Journal of Speech and Hearing Research, 19*, 290–296.

Repeated Measures Analysis of Variance

Independent Variables	1
Level of Measurement	Nominal
Number of Levels	2+
Number of Groups	1
Dependent Variables	**1**
Level of Measurement	Interval
Number of Levels	Many
Measurement Occasions	**2+**

Research Design

A repeated measures analysis of variance is used when there is just one group of people (or things) and they are measured several times on the same interval level dependent variable. The nominal independent variable is defined by the different measurement occasions. It can be one group measured across time or one group measured under different conditions. Repeated measures analysis of variance can be used when there are just two measurement occasions, but a **paired-samples *t* test** (see Module 17) is usually used in that situation, so, typically, for this analysis, there are at least three sets of scores compared.

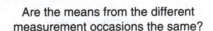

Are the means from the different measurement occasions the same?

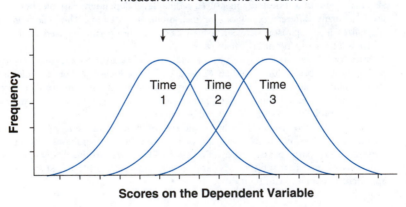

Scores on the Dependent Variable

Primary Statistical Question

Are the means from the several measurement occasions significantly different from each other?

Example of a Study That Would Use a Repeated Measures Analysis of Variance

There is a relationship between daily temperature and hospital admissions related to heart problems. Doctors wondered if this was because hot days stress the heart. One can "see" heart stress by measuring the presence of a chemical called a *B-type natriuretic peptide* or *BNP*. They designed a study where they measured the amount of BNP in the system of 92 patients on three occasions starting at the end of the summer. The first occasion was the hottest, the next occasion was a couple months later when it was mild, and the third measurement occasion was cool. With one group of people, a nominal independent variable with three levels (the three climate types) and an interval level dependent variable (*BNP* measured in particles per milliliter), a repeated measures analysis of variance, were used.

Analysis

The means and standard deviations (SD) from this study are shown:

	Hot		Mild		Cool	
	Mean	**SD**	**Mean**	**SD**	**Mean**	**SD**
Chemical	112.48	38.08	97.71	34.00	106.54	43.52

Repeated measures analyses of variance have two steps. In the first step, the group means are compared, and taking into account the standard deviations and correlational information across the measurement times, an *F* is produced with an associated level of significance. After a significant *F*, follow-up paired-samples *t* tests are performed for each pair of times to see where significant differences lie. In this study, there was an overall significant *F*, and follow-ups found that it was the drop from Time 1 to Time 2 that was significant, but other differences were not. A drop from hot weather to warm weather *was* associated with a decrease in stress on the heart.

Things to Consider

- Repeated measures analysis of variance is an extension of the paired-samples *t* test because it allows for analysis of more than two sets of scores. This is similar to how an **analysis of variance** (see Module 11) is an extension of the **independent *t* test** (see Module 8) to allow for more than two groups.
- Repeated measures analysis of variance works even if there are four, five, or more measurement occasions. As the number of measurement times gets large, though, the number of follow-up paired-samples *t* tests required gets unwieldy. In that case, when there are a lot of measurement times, **time series analysis** (see Module 23) becomes the stat for that.
- Any time means and standard deviations are used to judge whether different sets of scores are statistically different from each other the procedure is correctly called an analysis of variance. Researchers, though, when they hear "analysis of variance" will almost always picture independent groups being compared, not a repeated measures analysis like this one. Consequently, the comparison of multiple groups of people gets the shorter name of *analysis of variance*, while this repeated measures analysis is left with a much longer, more complicated name.

Real-Life Study That Inspired This Example

Wilker, E. H., Yeh, G., Wellenius, G. A., Davis, R. B., Phillips, R. S., & Mittleman, M. A. (2012). Ambient temperature and biomarkers of heart failure: A repeated measures analysis. *Environmental Health Problems, 120*(8), 1083–1087.

Two-Way Repeated Measures

Independent Variables	2+
Level of Measurement	Nominal
Number of Levels	2+
Number of Groups	2+
Dependent Variables	**1**
Level of Measurement	Interval
Number of Levels	Many
Measurement Occasions	**2+**

Research Design

This analysis is for designs where there are repeated measures grouped within other repeated measures. For example, people might be measured on three different days, and on each day they might be measured under three different conditions. Change might occur across time or across conditions or both. The two or more independent variables in this sort of study are nominal and represent different conditions or time periods. The single dependent variable is interval level and represents some variable that the research thinks might vary across the different time or conditions. If the overall test indicates that the dependent variable does differ across levels of one or more independent variables, follow-up **repeated measures analyses of variance** (see Module 20) are conducted to pinpoint where the differences lie.

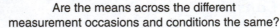

Are the means across the different
measurement occasions and conditions the same?

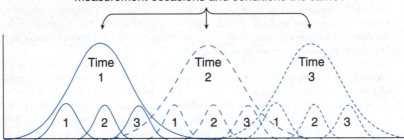

**Scores on the Dependent Variable for
Each Level of Each Independent Variable**

Primary Statistical Question

Are the means from the measurement occasions, as defined by either independent variable, significantly different from each other?

Example of a Study That Would Use a Two-Way Repeated Measures Analysis

Racehorses are trained with such great intensity that they are at risk for a variety of health issues specific to their profession. In fact, there is a whole veterinarian specialty dedicated to their health. A horse health researcher was interested in a particular chemical called fibrinogen that is associated with blood clotting and other cardiovascular problems. It was hypothesized that *omega-3*, an oil found in plants (and some seafood), if given to horses, would decrease the amount of fibrinogen in their blood. A study was designed with two independent variables representing two sets of conditions. The first independent variable was administering omega-3 every day for 30 days. This variable had two levels, Day 1 and Day 30. Because fibrinogen production decreases during a race, a second independent variable was included by measuring both before and after a practice race. The dependent variable was fibrinogen levels in the blood (measured as milligrams/deciliters). So on Day 1, the horses were measured twice, before and after the race. Then, after taking omega-3 for 30 days, they were again measured twice, before and after a race. It was assumed that, when combining data from both race days, fibrinogen levels would still decrease *during* a race, and the overall average fibrinogen level for the horses would also decrease during the 30 days of taking omega-3.

Analysis

The means and standard deviations for the two-way repeated measures analysis looked like this:

	Day 1				Day 30			
	Prerace		Postrace		Prerace		Postrace	
	Mean	SD	Mean	SD	Mean	SD	Mean	SD
Fibrinogen	158.20	12.56	157.8	10.72	130.60	6.58	117.80	11.30

The two-way repeated measures analysis produced a significant F for the 30 days of taking omega-3 ($F = 5.93$, $p = .04$) indicating that the overall levels of fibrinogen dropped after taking omega-3 for 30 days. This was true regardless of whether one measured the levels before or right after a race. The second independent variable (the effect of running in a race) turned out not to be significantly related to fibrinogen levels, all things considered. The researcher concluded that a diet that includes omega-3 would help lower horses' levels of this dangerous chemical.

Things to Consider

- A two-way repeated measures analysis also looks for *interactions* among the independent variables. This might be reflected in differences on the dependent variable related to one independent variable but only at certain levels of the other independent variable. In the example study's results, for instance, the difference in fibrinogen levels before and after a race was significant on Day 30 but was not on Day 1. The effect of racing (one independent variable) on the dependent variable (fibrinogen) depended on how long a horse had been taking omega-3 (the other independent variable). That indicates an interaction between the two independent variables.

Real-Life Study That Inspired This Example

Piccione, G., Marafioti, S., Giannetto, C., Panzera, M., & Fazio, F. (2014). Effect of dietary supplementation with omega 3 on clotting time, fibrinogen concentration and platelet aggregation in the athletic horse. *Livestock Science, 161,* 109–113.

Mixed Analysis of Variance

Independent Variables	2
Level of Measurement	Nominal
Number of Levels	2+
Number of Groups	2+
Dependent Variables	1
Level of Measurement	Interval
Number of Levels	Many
Measurement Occasions	2+

Research Design

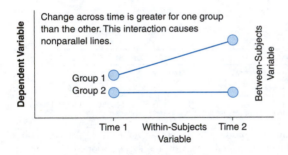

A mixed analysis of variance is called *mixed* because it both compares groups' means, like an analysis of variance, and compares change across time, like a repeated measures analysis. It has other names, as well. It is sometimes called a *mixed-models* analysis because of the different statistical models (mathematical equations) used in the analysis. A more complete label for the design is very long but describes this unusual design in detail: *An analysis of variance with one between-subjects variable and one within-subjects variable.* The between-subjects independent variable is nominal and defines the different groups of people. The within-subjects independent variable is nominal and defines the different measurement occasions or conditions. The dependent variable is at the interval level. The setup for a mixed analysis of variance looks very much like a **two-way analysis of variance** (see Module 12) with the possibility of an interaction being one of the research questions. Have all groups changed across time by the same amount? Interactions may be best understood visually. If you plot the mean scores on the dependent variable for each group at each point in time and connect the dots, you get lines showing the effect of the within-subjects variable on each group. If the effect of the within-subjects variable is the same regardless of which level of the between-subjects variable one is in, there is no interaction. If the lines are *not* parallel, there *is* an interaction.

Primary Statistical Questions

1. Is there an interaction between the *between-subjects* variable and the *within-subjects* variable?

2. Is there change over time for any group?

Example of a Study That Would Use a Mixed Analysis of Variance

Norway banned smoking indoors in restaurants in 2004. As part of a study, workers in the hospitality industry were assessed for respiratory symptoms right before the law was enacted and five months later. Researchers were also interested in how any effect might differ depending on whether the person was a smoker or nonsmoker. In this design the between-subjects nominal independent variable was whether one smoked or did not smoke, the within-subjects nominal independent variable was before or after the ban started, and the interval level dependent variable was an index of breathing problems where a lower number meant healthier lungs.

Analysis

Here are the data from the study. The top row represents smokers and the bottom row shows nonsmokers.

	Sample Size	Respiratory Index Before the Law	Respiratory Index After the Law	Change Over Time
Smokers	458	1.91	1.85	−.06
Nonsmokers	327	1.44	1.29	−.15

The analysis actually conducts several statistical tests. First, the primary question was whether there was improvement over time for everybody combined. There *was* significant improvement overall, $p \leq .001$. Second, there was an interaction, significant at the $p \leq .001$ level, as nonsmokers improved over time more than smokers. So, the ban seemed to have helped both types of workers in terms of respiratory health but helped nonsmokers more. A third analysis was also significant but not really of interest to the researchers. Unsurprisingly, the overall health of smokers was worse than nonsmokers, $p \leq .001$.

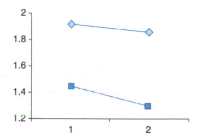

Things to Consider

- This "mixed-models" approach should not be confused with a "mixed-methods" approach that combines quantitative and qualitative research methods in the same study.
- Some books and journal articles use the term *repeated measures analysis of variance* to describe a mixed-models approach. The consensus, however, seems to be to use that broader term to describe a repeated measures analysis with just one group (and no between-subjects variable). This book follows that convention (see Module 20).
- The actual statistical test to identify an interaction is an analysis of variance on the average differences among groups at each point in time. If those differences are unequal between any two points in time, an interaction exists.

Real-Life Study That Inspired This Example

Eagan, T. M., Hetland, J., & Aarø, L. E. (2006). Decline in respiratory symptoms in service workers five months after a public smoking ban. *Tobacco Control, 15*(3), 242–246.

Time Series Analysis

Independent Variables	1
Level of Measurement	Nominal
Number of Levels	Many
Number of Groups	1
Dependent Variables	1
Level of Measurement	Interval
Number of Levels	Many
Measurement Occasions	2+

Research Design

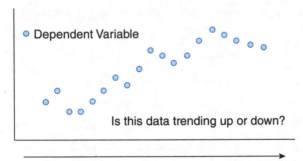

Sometimes in research, an interval level dependent variable is measured so frequently and regularly that a huge amount of information is available for analysis. One can determine whether the variable is changing over time with great power and precision. If there are many measurement occasions and the amount of time between the occasions is consistently the same, a time series analysis can be performed. The independent variable in a time series analysis is usually *time* (or, actually, the effect of some independent variable across time) and at *least* nominal, though it is almost always ordinal. An assumption in most statistical analyses is that the relationship between the independent variable and the dependent variable is linear. In other words, the expected pattern in time series analyses is that if values change over time they likely change in a straight line kind of way, either moving up or down. Consequently, the statistical analytic strategy is to see whether a particular line "fits" the data well. Another aspect of time series analysis is to control for *autocorrelation*. Autocorrelation is the idea that a score at any particular time is strongly related to (and best explained by) the score that came before it. Researchers, though, want to see what effect the independent variable of time has on the scores' variability and need to remove any of that variability that is due to other influences. So, time series analysis also controls for autocorrelation on those scores to try to isolate any influence of the independent variable on the dependent variable.

Primary Statistical Question

Is the dependent variable changing over time?

Example of a Study That Would Use a Time Series Analysis

In the 1970s, researchers in Philadelphia were interested in whether the rivers that fed the city's water supply were getting cleaner or more polluted. They measured levels of dissolved oxygen in the water (which is a good thing to have) every four days for a year.

Analysis

The data from the water analysis are shown here. The 91 points across time are along the bottom, and the possible dependent variable values (oxygen levels) are along the vertical axis.

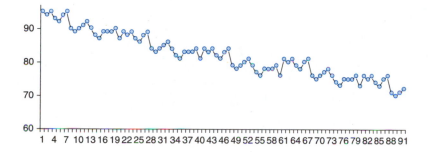

Among the statistical values used to interpret "trend lines" like the one shown in this example are an *R-squared*, which indicates the proportion of the variability in scores that is explained by a particular hypothesized line, and a *t* test or *F* test, which assesses whether there is, in fact, a significant change along the line. In the case of this data, there were significant findings, and it was concluded that the amount of oxygen in the water was decreasing predictably across time, which, in turn, suggested that Philadelphia's water pollution was getting worse.

Things to Consider

- Real-life data collected over time often form a pattern that isn't very smooth but instead rolls up and down like a wave. Following the linear relationship assumption, these variances away from a straight line are often treated as randomness or measurement error and some system of averaging adjacent values is used to straighten the line. This simplifying of the data is called *smoothing*. Smoothing is conceptually similar to using the means of groups instead of all the individual scores for *t* tests (see Module 8) and **analysis of variance** (see Module 11). For the same reason, sometimes scores are transformed mathematically in a standardized way to make the raw scores more closely fall on a straight line.
- Controlling for autocorrelation is very complex mathematically because not only is each score correlated with the score before it but also with the score before that one and all previous scores in the series. This is why you didn't see much time series analysis before the advent of easy-to-use computers.
- The approach used in time series analysis of trying to fit a hypothesized straight line onto data is the same strategy used in **simple linear regression** (see Module 32).

Real-Life Study That Inspired This Example

Fuller, F. C., Jr., & Tsokos, C. P. (1971). Time series analysis of water pollution data. *Biometrics, 27*(4), 1017–1034.

PART 4

CORRELATIONAL ANALYSES

This final collection of analyses involves calculating statistics to evaluate the strength of relationships among variables. For many of these procedures, researchers are only interested in how large the association between two variables is. For others, the goal is to actually predict or estimate the score on one variable by looking at the score on one or more other variables.

Most correlational designs have not randomly assigned subjects to groups (or different levels of a variable) to see whether they affect another variable. Without this design characteristic, one cannot determine whether one variable *causes* another. So, with correlational analyses, we hesitate to use the terminology of *dependent* and *independent* variables or language that suggests cause and effect. Instead, we refer to *criterion variables* to describe those variables we wish to understand, and we say *predictor variables* for those variables that we use to predict, estimate, or account for criterion variables.

Another common design feature for correlational analyses is that there is usually one big group of people (or things), and we collect scores for more than one variable from that group. We are not interested in differences between groups, but instead we are interested in associations between variables. For that reason, correlational analyses are sometimes described as being interested in relationships, while other statistics look for group differences. Most inferential statistics are interested in relationships between variables, though. It's just that if the independent variable happens to be at the nominal level, we end up comparing groups to see those relationships.

This section is organized into three groups. The first group of analyses involves one or more predictor variable and one criterion variable. A little later we present more powerful correlational analyses that have multiple predictors and multiple criterion variables. Then, at the end are three analyses that don't fit well into our simple descriptive strategy of only identifying the level of measurement of our predictor and criterion variables. These final three statistics use flexible variables that can be both predictor and criterion in the same analysis! As you might imagine, that leads to useful but somewhat more complicated procedures.

Kappa Coefficient of Agreement

Predictor Variables	0
Level of Measurement	—
Number of Levels	—
Number of Groups	1
Criterion Variables	1
Level of Measurement	Nominal
Number of Levels	2+
Measurement Occasions	2+

Research Design

The Kappa coefficient of agreement is a correlational analysis, but, unlike other correlational analyses, it is not interested in the relationship between two variables. This may sound odd because the word *correlation* means the relationship between two things. Here, though, the research design for which Kappa is used involves a variable that has been scored more than once or, most commonly, by more than one scorer or "judge." The relationship question is whether there is some association between the particular judge that assigned the rating and the score a person (or thing) received. Does it matter who does the scoring, or is there agreement among judges? Though the big fun table at the front of this book and the table at the start of this module describe the Kappa design as using no independent variables, you could think of the judges as the independent variable. Are the judges and the scores they've assigned consistent?

Questions of consistency in scoring are described by measurement folks as *reliability* concerns. Reliability is the extent to which a set of scores is random, and there are reliability statistics that determine how much of the variance in a group of scores is due to actual variability in the people (or things) being scored. Kappa is one of these statistics and is used when the scores are at the nominal level. Its value ranges from 0 to 1, and the closer to 1, the more agreement among judges. Kappa is used to estimate *interrater* (or interobserver) reliability.

Job Applicant	Judge A	Judge B	Judge C
Pierre	0	1	0
Manuel	2	2	1
Fatima	1	1	2
Jie	1	1	1

How much agreement is there among raters?

0 = Not Qualified, 1 = Qualified, 2 = Top Candidate

Primary Statistical Question

How consistent are scores across different judges or scoring methods?

Example of a Study That Would Use a Kappa Coefficient of Agreement

A researcher was concerned about an observational test of the movements that babies make. The subjective nature of the assessment meant that the scores might have poor interrater reliability. To estimate the test's reliability for a particular item (whether a child's gaze follows a pointed finger), two physicians categorized their observations of 53 babies on this item. The babies' success on this task was the nominal dependent variable and had four possible categories or scores.

Analysis

The quantitative information used to calculate Kappa is the number of judges and the number of possible scores. The number of people (or things) rated is important, too, but only until the various proportions used in the calculations are figured. A table showing the *frequencies* for all possible scoring permutations for this study is shown here and was used to determine Kappa.

Physician A's Scores	Physician B's Scores			
	1	2	3	4
1	**4**	2	2	0
2	3	**20**	4	0
3	1	3	**9**	1
4	0	0	1	**3**

The big bold values on a diagonal are the times that the two judges agreed. They agreed 68% of the time, but some of that percentage is expected. The formula for Kappa using this information resulted in a value of .51 (or 51%). There is a significance test available to tell us if .51 is greater than 0, but we know there will be some agreement no matter what. Instead, researchers interpret whether the Kappa value is big enough to suggest that there is adequate interrater reliability. One standard rule of thumb interprets Kappa this way: 0 to .40 is *poor*, .40 to .74 is *fair to good*, and .75 to 1.0 is *excellent*. So, the researcher concluded that interrater reliability for this part of the assessment was only fair.

Things to Consider

- The Kappa test works for any number of judges.
- Kappa is not the percentage of times judges agreed. It is the percentage of times judges agreed above and beyond what would be expected with a small number of options.
- Kappa only indicates whether raters tended to assign the same score to the same person, not whether the score is the right one to give. That's the difference between reliability and validity.
- Kappa can be used any time there are multiple scores for the same variable and can be used to look at consistency across time, not just as an estimate of interrater reliability.
- Kappa is not a person's name; it is a letter of the Greek alphabet. It is customarily capitalized because the symbol used for the kappa value is usually an upper case *K*.

Real-Life Article That Provided This Example

Haley, S. M., & Osberg, J. S. (1989). Kappa coefficient calculation using multiple ratings per subject: A special communication. *Physical Therapy, 69,* 970–974.

Spearman Correlation Coefficient

Predictor Variables	1
Level of Measurement	Ordinal
Number of Levels	Many
Number of Groups	1
Criterion Variables	1
Level of Measurement	Ordinal
Number of Levels	Many
Measurement Occasions	1

Research Design

The Spearman correlation coefficient is a statistic of *association*, which means that it tells us about the relationship between variables, not the difference between groups. It is similar to the **Pearson correlation coefficient** (see Module 31), but instead of looking at the association between two interval level variables, the Spearman correlation is between two ordinal level variables. The analytic strategy is to assign ranks to each of two variables and line them up side by side. By subtracting the ranks of one variable from the other, a bunch of difference scores are created. If the ranks for both variables are exactly the same, the difference scores will be all 0's. If there is a big difference between rankings, the difference scores are far from 0. A proportion ranging from 0 to 1 is created using that rank difference information and that proportion is then subtracted from 1. This final value is a Spearman correlation coefficient.

Participants	Rank Order on Test A	Rank Order on Test B	Rank Differences
Pierre	1	2	−1
Manuel	2	1	+1
Fatima	3	3	0
Jie	4	5	−1
Habib	5	4	+1
Jacob	6	8	−2
Liam	7	6	−1
Olivia	8	7	+1

This information is used to calculate the Spearman correlation coefficient.

Primary Statistical Question

How strongly are the two variables related?

Example of a Study That Would Use a Spearman Correlation Coefficient

Measurement experts in the social sciences like psychology and education are always concerned about the accuracy of their measurements. A common strategy when evaluating the usefulness of some new test or approach to measurement is to correlate scores from the new approach with an older accepted approach. If the scores correlate highly, one concludes that the new approach works well.

This strategy was used by researchers interested in the health of people living in neighborhoods. One accepted research finding is that the physical characteristics of a neighborhood affect the well-being of those who live there. For this sort of research, scientists walk the blocks of the neighborhood and measure various features and use these as variables to estimate the health of residents. It turns out that one of these variables that indicates health is trees. The more trees, the healthier the population. A new technique for assessing these physical features was suggested, which was using the photos found on web mapping services such as Google Street View. The research question was whether counting trees using this method was as valid as counting trees using the old *walking-around* method. They obtained data from the old-fashioned method on the number of trees on 37 streets and then compared that to the number of tree counts using the new-fangled street photo method. Because they weren't sure their variables of *number of trees* actually varied in a way that was interval level, they used a correlation method that only required ordinal level variables—the Spearman correlation coefficient.

Analysis

The researchers had 37 pairs of scores for their data. The Spearman correlation between number of trees counted using the old method and number of trees counted using the new method was significant and moderate in size, Spearman correlation coefficient (r_s) = .61, $p \leq .001$. Because the Spearman correlation's absolute value ranges from 0 to 1.0 and can be negative or positive, an interpretation of this correlation would be that the two methods seem to do just an *okay* job of measuring the same thing. It is likely that the street photo method (or, perhaps, the traditional method) misses some trees.

Things to Consider

- The scales and range of scores on the two different measures used for a Spearman correlational analysis need not be the same. Because the scores are transformed into ranks for the analysis they are placed onto the same scale before any computations, so any two sets of scores may be used. This is true for any correlation coefficient, such as the **phi correlation coefficient** (see Module 26) or the Pearson correlation, which is why correlations are such useful statistics.
- If there are more than just a few ties when creating ranks from a particular variable, there is an alternative formula for this test that corrects for that.
- The Spearman correlation is interpreted in the same way as a Pearson correlation coefficient. Additionally, if there are more than about 25 pairs of scores in the analysis the associated levels of significance are the same for both types of correlations.

Real-Life Study That Inspired This Example

Rundle, A. G., Bader, M. D. M., Richards, C. A., Neckerman, K. M., & Teitler, J. O. (2011). Using Google Street View to audit neighborhood environments. *American Journal of Preventive Medicine, 40*(1), 94–100.

Phi Correlation Coefficient

Predictor Variables	1
Level of Measurement	Nominal
Number of Levels	2
Number of Groups	1
Criterion Variables	1
Level of Measurement	Nominal
Number of Levels	2
Measurement Occasions	1

Research Design

The phi correlation coefficient quantifies the strength of the relationship between two nominal variables. It should be used when there are exactly two levels or categories in each of the variables.

When a researcher has measured one group of people (or things) on two different variables and they are at the nominal level, it is common to first conduct a **two-way chi-squared** test (see Module 6) to see if there is any association between the variables. That doesn't tell us the *effect size*, though. *Effect size* is the term for a quantity that indicates the strength of relationships among variables. Measures of association, like the phi correlation coefficient, are effect sizes. The phi ranges in value from -1.00 to 1.00, with values far from 0 indicating stronger relationships.

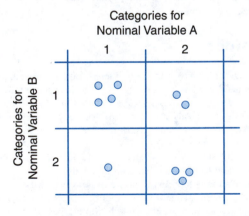

Categories for
Nominal Variable A

Is the category you're in on one variable related
to the category you're in on another variable?

Primary Statistical Question

How strongly are the two variables related?

Example of a Study That Would Use a Phi Correlation Coefficient

Are your two ears related to each other? More precisely, is there a correlation between people's hearing ability in one ear and the other? An otolaryngologist (ear, nose, and throat doctor) wondered this and designed a study. He tested 38 patients' left ears for whether they could hear a particularly difficult electronic tone and then tested their right ears as well. With the two nominal variables and exactly two categories for each (*left* or *right* ear and *yes* or *no* on whether patients could hear the tone), a phi correlation coefficient was the appropriate statistic to measure similarity between the ears.

Analysis

The results of the study, as frequencies of people in each category, are shown in this table:

	Yes	No
Right Ear	15	5
Left Ear	7	11

Often, researchers will run a two-way chi-squared first to see if there is any relationship between the variables and then follow-up with the phi correlation. The chi-squared analysis was significant, chi-squared = 5.07, p = .024. The phi correlation coefficient was .37, p = .024, indicating a moderate relationship. The two ears had similar hearing ability, but there was not great consistency between the two ears. Like some correlations, the phi correlation is directional, but because the variables are nominal, the "direction" is not usually interpreted. One can figure out the direction, though, if one knows how values were assigned in the statistical analysis. In this study, for example, 1's were used for *Yes's* and 2's were used for *No's*. Likewise, 1's were used for the right ear and 2's were used for the left ear. The positive correlation value means that those in the *higher* 2 category on one variable were more likely to be classified in the 2 category on the other variable. In other words, if an ear could not hear the tone, it was more likely to be the left ear than the right ear. Conversely, when the left ear was tested, it was more likely to not hear the tone. With correlations, we can always describe the relationship in two ways.

Things to Consider

- Though the math can be made to work for the phi when there are more than two categories in each variable, **Cramér's V coefficient** (see Module 27) works better for those situations.
- For this "2 by 2" design, the computed phi will be equal to the value of the Cramér's V coefficient.
- The significance for the phi correlation will always be the same as the significance for the results of the chi-squared analysis.
- There can be a perfect relationship between variables, and the value of phi still might not be 1.0. Though not common, this can happen sometimes when there are not an equal number of categories in each nominal variable.

Real-Life Study That Inspired This Example

Kuhn, G. M. (1973). The Phi coefficient as an index of ear differences in dichotic listening. *Cortex, 9,* 447–457.

Cramér's V Coefficient

Predictor Variables	1
Level of Measurement	Nominal
Number of Levels	2+
Number of Groups	1
Criterion Variables	1
Level of Measurement	Nominal
Number of Levels	2+
Measurement Occasions	1

Research Design

Cramér's V coefficient test produces a correlation coefficient between two nominal level variables. It is more commonly used than the **Phi correlation coefficient** (see Module 26) because it can be used with any number of categories or levels in the two variables, not just two. Like all correlation coefficients, Cramér's V coefficient is an *effect size*, which means it is an estimate of the strength of a relationship among variables. It ranges from 0 to 1.0, and the closer it is to 1.0, the stronger the association. In practice, Cramér's V usually comes after a **two-way chi-squared** analysis (see Module 6). The two-way chi-squared indicates that there *is* a relationship between two nominal variables, and Cramér's V tells you how strong that relationship is. It could also be used as a preliminary step for a **multiple logistic regression** (see Module 29) to identify good candidates to use as predictors.

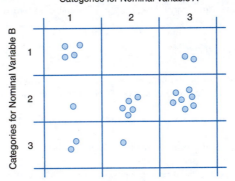

Is the category you're in on one variable related to the category you're in on another variable?

Primary Statistical Question

How strongly are the two variables related?

Example of a Study That Would Use a Cramér's V Coefficient

Are you happier in a management job if you have moved up in the organization over time, or can you be just as satisfied staying at the same management level with the same responsibilities? A researcher surveyed 286 managers at different levels in a huge corporation and, among other things, asked them if they were satisfied with their job (*yes* or *no*) and how often they had been promoted or given responsibilities that reflected a promotion. The promotion variable was thought of as *upward mobility* and coded as three categories reflecting the amount of mobility experienced (*minimum*, *moderate*, and *maximum*). With two variables that were nominal (and, actually, mobility is coded as an ordinal level variable), Cramér's V was computed to see the strength of the relationship.

Analysis

The number of managers in each category on the two variables is shown in this table:

	Upward Mobility		
	Minimum	Moderate	Maximum
Satisfied	11	32	18
Unsatisfied	101	94	30

A two-way chi-squared was computed first to see if any relationship existed. It was significant, chi-squared = 17.8, $p \leq .001$. The related Cramér's V was .25, $p \leq .001$. One interprets V as any other correlation coefficient, so .25 indicates only a small to moderate relationship. Those with few promotions were likely to be unsatisfied, but there was a tendency to be unsatisfied at this company regardless of how upwardly mobile one has been.

Things to Consider

- Like all correlation coefficients, Cramér's V looks like a proportion, but it is not. We do not refer to a Cramér's V coefficient of .45 as 45%.
- The calculations for Cramér's V are based on the two-way chi-squared analysis for the data, along with the number of categories in the two variables. Consequently, the level of significance of Cramér's V will be the same as the chi-squared's significance.
- If there are exactly two categories in each variable, Cramér's V coefficient is the same as the Phi correlation coefficient one could compute. This suggests that there is really no need to ever use the Phi, except perhaps for tradition's sake. Many textbooks and software programs suggest that one should use Phi *instead* of Cramér's V when there are exactly two categories in each variable, but the reason for this is unclear. Perhaps it is because researchers are more familiar with the Phi.
- Cramér's V is always a positive number, but it is not correct to think of a relationship between two nominal variables as positive or negative the way one does with the **Pearson correlation coefficient** (see Module 31). If the Cramér's V coefficient is used for ordinal level variables, however, as it often is, researchers sometimes use "positive" or "negative" as descriptors, even though the value itself is never negative.

Real-Life Study That Inspired This Example

Grusky, O. (1966). Career mobility and organizational commitment. *Administrative Science Quarterly, 10*(4), 488–503.

Simple Logistic Regression

Predictor Variables	1
Level of Measurement	Nominal+
Number of Levels	2+
Number of Groups	1
Criterion Variables	1
Level of Measurement	Nominal
Number of Levels	2
Measurement Occasions	1

Research Design

The most common design for which simple logistic regression is appropriate has one predictor variable and a single criterion variable, both usually at the nominal level with just two levels. The term *simple* indicates there is only one independent variable; it is usually nominal, but it need not be. Interval level variables can be used as predictors as well. Data are collected for both variables from one large group of people, almost always at the same time.

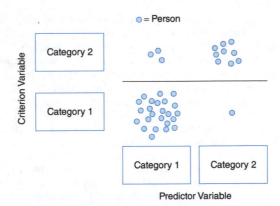

Primary Statistical Question

For those at each level (or at each score or in each category) of the independent variable, what are the probabilities that they will be in a given category on the dependent variable?

Example of a Study That Would Use Simple Logistic Regression

A survey was administered to 1,431 inhabitants of a seaside community. As an independent variable, the amount of fish eaten regularly was assessed ("Think of all the meals you eat in a week; how many usually include fish?"). To simplify interpretation, the researchers chose a "cut score" on this independent variable and created a nominal independent variable with two levels. In this example, the researcher decided that the key point on the independent variable was whether villagers ate two or more fish meals a week. Anything less than that, and they were "infrequent fish eaters." As a dependent variable, the survey included items from a depression measure. Scores above an accepted point on the depression scale were interpreted as indicating depression.

Analysis

Assume the study produced the data in this table.

	Number of Fish Meals Each Week	
	0 or 1	More Than 1
Depressed	34	137
Not Depressed	160	1,100

After creating two groups of people, "frequent fish eaters" and "infrequent fish eaters," statistical analysis resulted in an *odds ratio* of 1.41 for infrequent fish eaters. The odds ratio indicates the probability of being in the depressed group for infrequent fish eaters compared to frequent fish eaters. An odds ratio of 1.0 would mean there is no difference in likelihood of being depressed between the two groups. The odds ratio of 1.4, which was statistically significant, means that our best guess about those who eat a low amount of fish each week is that they are 41 percent more likely to be depressed compared to those who eat a larger amount of fish.

Things to Consider

- When the independent variable is at the interval level, the odds ratio indicates the increased or decreased probability of membership in the target category for every increase of 1 point on the independent variable.
- Simple logistic regression has the same design as a **discriminant analysis** (see Module 30) if the dependent variable for the discriminant analysis has only two levels. Which procedure one chooses depends on the type of information one wishes to get in the output.
- When there is only one independent variable and it is nominal, researchers often use a **two-way chi-squared** test (see Module 6) instead of logistic regression because of its simplicity.
- When there is more than one predictor variable in logistic regression, **multiple logistic regression** (see Module 29) is used. Also, if the dependent variable has more than two categories, one uses a procedure known as *multinomial logistic regression.*
- The data are often graphed in a way that produces a probability curve. As one moves along the scores on the independent variable on the X-axis, what is the probability of placement in the selected group on the dependent variable? The typical jump at a certain point on the X-axis creates the common shape known as the *logistic curve.*

Real-Life Study That Inspired This Example

Tanskanen, A., Hibbeln, J. R., Tuomilehto, J., Uutela, A., Haukkala, A., Viinamaki, H., et al. (2001). Fish consumption and depressive symptoms in the general population in Finland. *Psychiatric Services, 52,* 529–531.

Multiple Logistic Regression

Predictor Variables	2+
Level of Measurement	Nominal+
Number of Levels	2+
Number of Groups	1
Criterion Variables	1
Level of Measurement	Nominal
Number of Levels	2
Measurement Occasions	1

Research Design

Multiple logistic regression is appropriate when one has two or more predictors and a single criterion variable at the nominal level with just two levels. The term *multiple* indicates there is more than one predictor. The predictors can be nominal or higher or a mix of levels, but interpretation in logistic regression is a bit easier when predictors are nominal and each has just two levels. Data are collected for all variables, usually at the same time, from one large group of people.

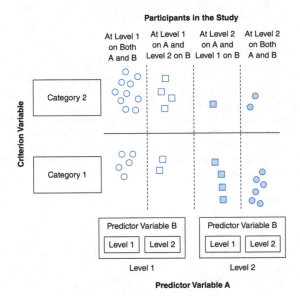

Primary Statistical Question

For those at each level (or each score or in each category) of the independent variables, what are the probabilities that they will be in a given category on the dependent variable?

Example of a Study That Would Use Multiple Logistic Regression

Researchers were interested in the dangers of tanning in terms of the risk of getting skin cancer. They recruited two types of people, those who had skin cancer and those who did not, and formed one large group. Two independent variables that should theoretically be risk factors for skin cancer were chosen and measured at the nominal level with two levels. They were *type of job* (outdoors or indoors) and *ability to tan* (good tanners or bad tanners). The dependent variable of *presence or absence of skin cancer* was nominal with two levels.

Analysis

As with **simple logistic regression** (see Module 28), results for multiple logistic regression are typically formatted in terms of *odds ratios* for ease of interpretation. *Odds ratios* indicate the odds of being at a given level on the dependent variable for those in a given category of each independent variable. With multiple predictors, the odds ratios are calculated for each predictor, often holding the other predictors constant so the independent contributions of each predictor can be seen. (This is similar to the way **multiple linear regression** works [see Module 33] in controlling for all other predictors when calculating each independent variable's predictive weight.) Imagine the results of this study looked like this:

Independent Variable	Odds Ratio	95% Confidence Interval
People with outdoor jobs	1.77	.86–4.03
Bad tanners	2.20	1.61–3.20

Notice that, for simplicity, only the particular level or category of each independent variable that the researcher believes is critical to making a difference is shown. An odds ratio is calculated for that level. As with all inferential statistics, there is an assumed range of true population values of odds ratios within which the sample value falls. Most logistic regression analyses calculate that range, shown as a *95% confidence interval*, for each odds ratio. An odds ratio of 1.0 indicates no relationship between a predictor and the criterion, so if the confidence interval includes a 1.0, the associated odds ratio is not statistically significant. Consequentially, the interpretation for these results would be that whether one works outdoors makes no difference in the development of skin cancer. Having skin that does not tan well, however, makes one more than twice as likely to develop skin cancer (the odds ratio is 2.2).

Things to Consider

- Multiple logistic regression has the same design as a **discriminant analysis** (see Module 30) if the dependent variable for the discriminant analysis has only two levels. Which procedure one chooses depends on the type of information one wishes to get in the output.
- When there is only one predictor variable in logistic regression, the analysis is referred to as **simple logistic regression** (see Module 28).
- A form of logistic regression exists for when the dependent variable has more than two categories. That procedure is called *multinomial logistic regression*.

Real-Life Study That Inspired This Example

Dubin, N., Moseson, M., & Pasternack, B. S. (1989). Sun exposure and malignant melanoma among susceptible individuals. *Environmental Health Perspectives, 81,* 139–151.

Discriminant Analysis

Independent Variables	2+
Level of Measurement	Nominal+
Number of Levels	2+
Number of Groups	1
Dependent Variables	1
Level of Measurement	Nominal
Number of Levels	2+
Measurement Occasions	1

Research Design

Discriminant analysis is used when the researcher wishes to look at the relationships between independent variables and a single nominal dependent variable by seeing how well the independent variables can correctly classify people or things into the groups that represent the dependent variable. One or more independent variables (or *predictors*) at any level of measurement are used to guess in which category each person (or thing) should be placed. Data are collected for all variables from one large group of people, usually at the same time.

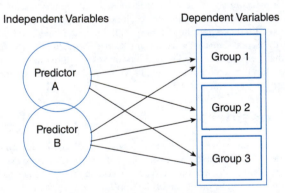

Do scores on the independent variables predict which groups a person is in?

Primary Statistical Questions

How useful is each predictor in accurately classifying people (or things) into each level of the dependent variable? How accurate is the overall classification?

Example of a Study That Would Use Discriminant Analysis

Six hundred twenty college freshmen were tracked for ten years to see if they 1) graduated, 2) dropped out for academic reasons, or 3) dropped out for nonacademic reasons. Researchers were interested in whether grade point average after the first year or their incoming SAT scores would help predict their eventual success. Final graduation or dropout status was the three-category dependent variable, and SAT scores and freshman GPA were the two interval level independent variables.

Analysis

Interpretation of discriminant analysis results focuses on the relative contribution of each predictor variable. Linear composites called *functions* are created (similar to the linear equations created in **multiple linear regression** [see Module 33] or the factors produced in **exploratory factor analysis** [see Module 35]). When more than two predictor variables are used, or the dependent variable has more than two categories, discriminant analysis produces more than one function. Each function represents a different way that people differ across groups. In this example, we only show and interpret the first function (which is the one that does the best job of classification).

	Function #1
SAT	.359
First-year GPA	1.017

Of the original cases, 48.4% were correctly classified.

In this analysis, *first-year grade point average* is more strongly related to eventual success in college than is performance on the *SAT* (GPA's standardized weight, 1.02, is about three times as big as SAT's weight of .36). Using these predictors, we were able to place students into the three groups with 48.4% accuracy. To see if this is a good hit rate, we need to compare that percentage to the percentage in the largest group (because if we knew nothing, our best guess would be to go with the biggest group). In this study, the naturally occurring percentages in the three groups were 50% graduated, 29% academic dropout, and 21% nonacademic dropout. Because 48.4% is less than 50%, using these variables by themselves would not improve our identification of at-risk students.

Things to Consider

- Discriminant analysis is also called *discriminant function analysis.*
- Discriminant analysis differs from **multiple logistic regression** (see Module 29) because the dependent variable can have more than two categories or levels.
- If the dependent variable starts out nice and continuous at the interval level, it is likely best to use **multiple linear regression** instead of losing information by forcing the dependent variable into just a few categories.
- Do not confuse discriminant analysis with **cluster analysis** (see Module 37), which *creates* groups. Discriminant analysis examines groups that already exist.
- A discriminant analysis can be flipped and a **multivariate analysis of variance** (see Module 14) can be used. Then, the independent variables become dependent variables and the dependent variable becomes the independent variable. The research question then becomes whether the independent variable groups' means differ for any of the dependent variables. Notice this is a different research question than the question of accurate classification.

Pearson Correlation Coefficient

Predictor Variables	1
Level of Measurement	Interval
Number of Levels	Many
Number of Groups	1
Criterion Variables	1
Level of Measurement	Interval
Number of Levels	Many
Measurement Occasions	1

Research Design

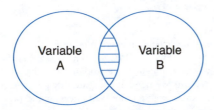

Two variables are correlated when people tend to score about the same on them.

The Pearson correlation coefficient is the granddaddy of statistics. It's older than all the others, developed in the late 1800s to scale the relationship between two variables in a standardized easy-to-interpret way. The design for all correlation coefficients, including the Pearson, involves a single group of people (or things) that are measured on exactly two variables. It is the correlation to use when both variables are at the interval level. Because scientists usually try to measure their variables at the interval level, the Pearson correlation coefficient is widely used, taught early, and even somewhat familiar to the general public.

Pearson correlation coefficients range from −1.0 to +1.0, and the math works in a clever way to give us two pieces of information about the nature of the relationship between the two variables. The absolute value (ignoring the minus or plus sign) reflects the *strength* of the relationship. Correlations close to 0 indicate a weak association between variables. Correlations far from 0, whether negative or positive, indicate a strong association. The negative or positive sign indicates the *direction* of the relationship. A correlation is positive, and said to have a positive direction, when the one-to-one relationship among the pairs of scores is such that one who scores *high* on one variable is likely to score *high* on the other and one who scores *low* on one is likely to score *low* on the other. A correlation is negative when those scoring high on one variable tend to score low on the other and vice versa. Keep in mind, though, that a negative correlation can still be high and strong. It is the number itself that tells us the strength of the relationship.

Primary Statistical Question

How strongly, and in what direction, are the two variables related?

Example of a Study That Would Use a Pearson Correlation Coefficient

Income has been found to be related to one's health. Those with less money tend to be less healthy. For those who study communities and have to plan for providing health services, the income level for those in a neighborhood might be a clue as to the health needs of its residences. To see if this relationship was strong enough to use for health services planning, data were collected from 100 neighborhoods in Sheffield, England. Two interval level variables were correlated. An index of poverty that included the percentage of households in the neighborhood that received government assistance and the percentage of people who did not own property was one variable. The other variable was the percentage of people in the neighborhood who chose "not good health" on England's national census survey.

Analysis

A Pearson correlation for the 100 neighborhoods' pairs of scores was calculated. It was .85, and significant, $p \leq .001$, which indicates a strong and positive relationship between the two variables. In other words, poverty as a variable can be used in this context to estimate health pretty well. Because of how health was measured, *high* poverty meant *high* chance of poor health. As an *effect size* (a value indicating strength of relationships among variables), the size of the Pearson correlation coefficient was more important than its significance level.

Things to Consider

- The Pearson correlation is not a proportion, though it looks like one, especially when it is positive. If you square a Pearson correlation, however, you do get a proportion. It is the proportion of shared variance between the two variables, or the proportion of variance in one variable accounted for by the other, or the amount of shared information, or (to use the image of a Pearson correlation as two overlapping circles) the proportion of overlap between the two variables.
- The full name for the Pearson correlation coefficient, which many textbooks and professors like to use, is the *Pearson product moment correlation*. A "moment" in mathematics is a number that describes a set of values. For example, one moment is the sum of all the values. Another moment, called the *first* moment, is the mean of the values, and when *moment* is used by itself, it refers to the mean. The correlation coefficient is (to simplify a bit) calculated by multiplying all the pairs of scores together and then averaging those cross-products. This results in a *product moment* correlation.
- Pearson correlations reflect consistency. So, they can be used to estimate *reliability* in a set of scores to see how much randomness there is in a testing or measurement approach.
- There are two sets of standards for interpreting correlations. In most social science fields, this rule of thumb is used: 0 to .30 = small, .30 to .50 = medium, and .50 and above = large. In measurement, as evidence of validity or reliability, these standards are used: 0 to .30 = small, .30 to .70 = medium, and .70 and above = large.
- Correlations with a positive sign are referred to as positive relationships, whether or not, of course, they suggest a *good* or *bad* thing. For example, the "positive" relationship between income level and poor health is probably nothing to feel good about.

Real-Life Study That Inspired This Example

Alwan, N., Wilkinson, M., Birks, D., & Wright, J. (2007). Do standard measures of deprivation reflect health inequities in older people? *Journal of Public Health Policy, 28*(3), 356–362.

Simple Linear Regression

Predictor Variables	1
Level of Measurement	Interval
Number of Levels	Many
Number of Groups	1
Criterion Variables	1
Level of Measurement	Interval
Number of Levels	Many
Measurement Occasions	1 or 2

Research Design

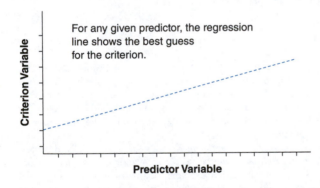

For any given predictor, the regression line shows the best guess for the criterion.

Simple linear regression uses one variable to guess how people would score on another variable. Its research design is the same as that for a **Pearson correlation coefficient** (see Module 31), and the Pearson correlation is the heart of a simple linear regression analysis. Data are collected from one group on two interval level variables and a correlation is calculated. Then, though, a procedure is used to estimate or predict what the score would be on some *criterion variable* by knowing the score on some *predictor variable*. Researchers use simple linear regression in two situations. Sometimes they want to predict a score in the future, such as administrators looking at students' high school performance to guess what their college grade point averages will be. Other times researchers are interested in exploring the relationship between two variables to understand them better. Under the first scenario, we tend to say that we are *predicting* scores. Under the second scenario, we are *estimating* scores.

The strategy for regression is to create an equation that uses the correlation coefficient and information about the two sets of scores (their means and variability). The equation allows us to pop in any predictor score and get a guess for what the criterion score will be. The equation is such that if you plotted all the possible guesses for the criterion against all the possible scores on the predictor and connected the dots, you'd get a straight line. So, we call the regression procedure *linear* and the line is called a *regression line*. Our guesses fall along that line.

Primary Statistical Question

How accurate are our guesses using the regression equation?

Example of a Study That Would Use Simple Linear Regression

Colleges don't have enough room for every high school student who applies, and admissions offices must use some information to try to guess who will succeed in order to make their decisions. One popular predictor has always been SAT scores. In the late 1960s, as the college population was changing, researchers were interested in what the actual linear relationship was between scores on the verbal section of the SAT, an interval level variable that ranged from 200 to 800, and college grade point average (GPA) for the first year, which ranged from 0.00 to 4.00. They collected data on both variables from a sample of about 4,000 students.

Analysis

Simple linear regression produces an equation that uses the predictor variable to predict the criterion variable. The equation includes some *constant* (a starting value based on the mean and variability of both variables) and a *weight* that is multiplied with the predictor variable's score. In this study, there was a .48 correlation between the SAT verbal score and eventual first-year college GPA, which suggested that it should be a pretty good predictor. The following regression equation was calculated:

$$\text{Predicted GPA} = -.667 + (.0051 \times \text{SAT Verbal score})$$

Admissions officers could use the equation to predict first-year GPA using SAT Verbal scores. For example, if an applicant reported an SAT Verbal score of 500, the math looks like this:

$$-.667 + (.0051 \times 500)$$

$$-.667 + (2.55) = 1.88$$

So, 1.88 would be the best guess for that student's first-year GPA. This was back when the average college student got C's. The average college GPA is quite a bit higher than that now.

Things to Consider

- If both variables are standardized to have the same mean and variability, the *weight* for the predictor variable will be the Pearson correlation coefficient for the two variables.
- When researchers are hoping to generalize their findings to describe a general relationship between variables, they will sometimes remove a few *outliers* from their sample in order to not be misled by the eccentricities of the sample they happen to be using. Outliers are participants whose predicted scores are very far away from the regression line that describes the relationship for most people in the sample.
- *Regression* means to return to some central value. A regression line is made up of the average criterion scores as estimated by the correlation between the predictor and criterion variables. Though the prediction will actually be wrong for most scores, on average your best strategy for guessing any given criterion variable score is to "return" to that regression line.
- The word *simple* as used by statisticians usually means "one." For example, *simple* linear regression uses exactly one predictor variable.

Real-Life Study That Inspired This Example

Cleary, T. A. (1968). Test bias: Prediction of grades of Negro and White students in integrated colleges. *Journal of Educational Measurement, 5*(2), 115–124.

<h1>MODULE 33</h1>

MODULE 33

Multiple Linear Regression

Predictor Variables	2+
Level of Measurement	Interval
Number of Levels	Many
Number of Groups	1
Criterion Variables	1
Level of Measurement	Interval
Number of Levels	Many
Measurement Occasions	1

Research Design

Multiple regression controls for the redundant, overlapping information among predictors, building an equation that reflects the pure, independent relationships of each predictor with the criterion.

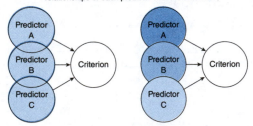

Less accurate, weaker prediction   More accurate, stronger prediction

Multiple linear regression is similar to **simple linear regression** (see Module 32), except that it uses the scores from more than one predictor variable to estimate a criterion variable. Scores are collected from one group of people (or things) on more than one interval level predictor variable and on one interval level criterion variable. The result of multiple linear regression is a regression equation that uses all predictor variables to predict the criterion variable. The math works cleverly to find the equation that works the best and makes guesses that correlate as strongly as possible with the actual criterion scores. The equation produced in multiple linear regression includes each predictor variable multiplied by an associated weight. When that weight is standardized, it is called a *Beta weight*. Beta weights show the independent contribution of each predictor to (or independent *relationship with*) the criterion variable. In this way, multiple regression gives us different and better information than we would get if we just took each predictor and correlated it with the criterion. Multiple regression not only usually improves the accuracy of prediction over using a single predictor but also allows us to compare each predictor to other predictors to see their relative importance, conceptually and practically speaking.

Primary Statistical Question

What are the relative contributions of each predictor to the criterion variable?

Example of a Study That Would Use Multiple Linear Regression

Psychological researchers were interested in which factors in a child's life predicted (or were related to) quality of life. Several measures were given to 364 children and their parents to allow for a multiple regression with four interval level predictor variables (child's *mental health problems*, child's *social skills*, level of *social support* from the family, number of *stressful life events*) and one interval level criterion variable (child's *quality of life* as defined by health, number of friends, success in school, and emotional functioning).

Analysis

Multiple regression produces a *multiple correlation coefficient,* or *multiple R*, which is the correlation between the predicted criterion scores and the actual criterion scores. The multiple R in this study was .47, indicating a moderate relationship between the four predictors and quality of life. To allow for a comparison among predictors, Beta weights are calculated in the table.

The best predictor with quality of life was the child's *mental health problems*. The negative weight means that the fewer of those, the higher the child's *quality of life*. The relationship between quality of life and social skills was significant and positive, while the number of stressful life events was negatively related to quality of life. Notice in

Predictor	Beta Weight
Mental health problems	−.81*
Social skills	.17*
Social support	.01
Stressful life events	−.14*

*p < .05

this mix of predictors that social support did not contribute to quality of life. This doesn't mean that it is not important, but the information it provides might already be accounted for by other predictors. The researchers interpreted these results as meaning that mental health plays a role that is about four or five times as important as *social skills* or *stressful life events* in explaining quality of life.

Things to Consider

- With a single predictor, the standardized weight for a predictor will be the Pearson correlation coefficient. With multiple predictors, though, that is not the case. The standardized Beta weights indicate the *independent* relationship with the criterion after accounting for (controlling for, "removing") each predictor's relationship with *other predictors*. Because predictors almost always are related to each other, Beta weights will not be the same as whatever the Pearson correlation between a predictor and the criterion is.
- The predictive formulas produced in multiple linear regression are such that *multiple R* is always positive. If you square it, you will get the proportion of variance on the criterion variable explained by the combination of the predictor variables.
- **Canonical correlation** (see Module 34) is multiple regression with more than one criterion variable.

Real-Life Study That Inspired This Example

Bastiaansen, D., Koot, H. M., & Ferdinand, R. F. (2005). Determinants of quality of life in children with psychiatric disorders. *Quality of Life Research, 14*(6), 1599–1612.

Canonical Correlation

Independent Variables	2+
Level of Measurement	Interval
Number of Levels	Many
Number of Groups	1
Dependent Variables	**2+**
Level of Measurement	Interval
Number of Levels	Many
Measurement Occasions	**1**

Research Design

Canonical correlation is used when the researcher wishes to look at the relationships between several interval level independent variables and several interval level dependent variables. Somewhat similar to **multiple linear regression** (see Module 33), which sees how well a linear composite of predictor variables can explain a single criterion variable, canonical correlation sees how well a linear composite of predictor variables can explain a linear composite of criterion variables. Think of whatever the predictor variables have in common as a variable of its own. How strongly is that variable related to whatever the several criterion variables have in common? Canonical correlation is most often used when an abstract criterion variable can't be measured well with a single score or measurement strategy.

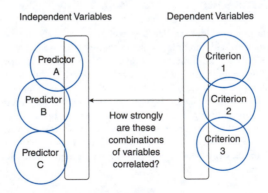

How much does each variable
contribute to its linear composite?

Primary Statistical Question

How strongly are the predictor variables related to the criterion variables?

Example of a Study That Would Use Canonical Correlation

One researcher believed that a good teacher should value the principles of John Dewey, a twentieth-century philosopher, who believed that students should have some say in their own learning. Which personality characteristics are associated with this value system? Three measures that represent this philosophy were identified, two different attitude surveys and a measure of how flexible one is in his or her own beliefs. Scores on these measures were chosen as dependent or criterion variables. The independent (or predictor) variables were three personality traits (*emotional vs. rational*, *imaginative vs. practical*, and *experimenting vs. conservative*).

Analysis

Canonical correlation finds the best combination of predictors that correlates as highly as possible with the best combination of the criterion variables. This combination is a *canonical function*. Many functions can be identified, but, often, only the first function is significant and interpreted, and that is the function shown here. Imagine the results looked like this.

		Standardized Weight
Predictor Variables	Emotional	.345
	Imaginative	.462
	Experimenting	.508
Criterion Variables	Dewey Beliefs Test 1	.748
	Dewey Beliefs Test 2	.533
	Flexibility	.195

The weights are the weights on the equations that define the two linear combinations of variables. They can be compared to each other to see the relative contribution of each variable. Assuming that the overall correlation and each weight are statistically significant, it appears that a Dewey philosophy (as defined mostly by the first Dewey beliefs test) correlates with the personality traits of experimenting, imaginative, and being emotional.

Things to Consider

- As with **multiple linear regression**, canonical correlation can include nominal variables. They are recoded as *dummy variables*, variables with just two levels (or *dichotomous*) that represent a single category of the nominal variable.
- Because there can be a large number of independent variables and a large number of dependent variables, many other statistical procedures can be thought of as specific examples of canonical correlation.
- Canonical correlation is a *multivariate* approach, which means that statistical analyses are made not on matching pairs of single variables but on the combinations of multiple outcome variables. As such, it capitalizes on what is probably a more accurate and meaningful measurement of the often fuzzy concepts researchers wish to use as variables.

Real-Life Study That Inspired This Example

Elmore, R. F., & Ellett, C. D. (1978). A canonical analysis of personality characteristics, personal and teaching practice beliefs, and dogmatism of beginning teacher education students. *Journal of Experimental Education, 47*(2), 112–117.

Exploratory Factor Analysis

Predictor Variables	2+
Level of Measurement	Interval
Number of Levels	Many
Number of Groups	1
Criterion Variables	2+
Level of Measurement	Interval
Number of Levels	Many
Measurement Occasions	1

Research Design

Correlations among A, B, and C and among D, E, and F suggest that two unmeasured *latent* factors account for the six measured variables.

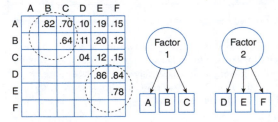

	A	B	C	D	E	F
A		.82	.70	.10	.19	.15
B			.64	.11	.20	.12
C				.04	.12	.15
D					.86	.84
E						.78
F						

Like other statistics toward the end of the Correlational Analyses section, exploratory factor analysis involves looking at the correlations among a bunch of interval level variables. With this procedure, the specific goal is to reveal the invisible unmeasured theoretical variables that explain those correlations. The idea is that when we have a lot of different scores representing what we think are many different variables, there may actually be just a few variables that are reflected by the many different scores. Statisticians call these theoretical underlying factors *latent variables*. *Latent* means hidden. If several measured variables correlate together, maybe they all really represent a single variable that we just didn't happen to (or couldn't) measure directly. The strategy is to interpret a correlation among variables as evidence that they measure the same thing. There are two common reasons that researchers perform exploratory factor analyses. Generally, exploratory factor analysis is used to understand the relationships among many variables in order to build a theory or conceptual model of those variables and the world. Measurement folks, though, also use exploratory factor analysis to help decide which questions or items on a test they are developing should go together and be combined as a single score that represents some single variable.

Primary Statistical Question

What factors best explain an observed pattern of correlations among variables?

Example of a Study That Would Use Exploratory Factor Analysis

What do you do when you have been hurt by someone? A researcher asked that question of 1,030 people and suggested six responses to consider. For each response offered, participants were asked to rate on a 7-point scale (1 = very unlikely to 7 = very likely) how likely they were to react in this way. The scores on all six variables (those options to consider) were correlated together, and those correlations were used to conduct an exploratory factor analysis. Were there a few underlying factors that accounted for scores on the six options?

Analysis

The results of an exploratory factor analysis are shown as a table of possible factors with the loadings for each variable on each factor shown. A loading is a standardized value (-1.0 to +1.0) that shows how strongly each variable is related to each factor. Those variables with high loadings help us figure out how to define and name that factor. The analysis for this study suggested two factors with these loading for each of the six items:

What Do You Do When You Are Hurt?	Factor 1	Factor 2
I try to overlook it.	.63	.12
I try to forgive so I will feel better.	.55	.23
I try to forgive because it is the decent thing to do.	.50	.15
I discuss it with them.	.19	.51
I ask for the other's forgiveness.	.14	.46
I apologize to them.	.03	.35

Notice that three variables correlate highly with *Factor 1* but fairly weakly with *Factor 2*, and three variables correlate highly with *Factor 2* but not so much with *Factor 1*. These fairly "clean" loadings suggest that there are two ways of responding when hurt. Factor 1 is an *internal* way of reacting, while Factor 2 involves *interacting with the person* who caused the pain, such as talking with them or apologizing.

Things to Consider

- Because there are many acceptable ways of finding factors and quantifying how well each variable "loads" on a factor, there are many subjective decisions that statisticians must make along the way. These choices are based on assumptions about what sort of factor model is best. Consequently, factor analysis is part art and part science.
- Exploratory factor analysis looks at patterns of relationships among real-world scores to build theories about unseen variables. **Confirmatory factor analysis** (see Module 36) does the opposite. It starts with a theory about unseen variables and wants to see if the patterns of relationships among real-world scores are consistent with that theory.
- Though there are ways of determining the statistical significance of a factor and factor loadings, they are not often used when making decisions in exploratory factor analysis.
- In some software packages, like SPSS, factor analysis is found under a "Data Reduction" menu option because of its goal of reducing the number of variables one needs to discuss.

Real-Life Study That Inspired This Example

Gorsuch, R. L., & Hao, J. Y. (1993). An exploratory factor analysis and its relationships to religious variables. *Review of Religious Research, 34*(4), 333–347.

Confirmatory Factor Analysis

Predictor Variables	2+
Level of Measurement	Interval
Number of Levels	Many
Number of Groups	1
Criterion Variables	2+
Level of Measurement	Interval
Number of Levels	Many
Measurement Occasions	1

Research Design

Confirmatory factor analysis starts with a theory, or what statisticians call a *model*, about the relationships among variables and then checks to see whether actual data from the real world correlate together as theory expects it to. In a way, it is the opposite of **exploratory factor analysis** (see Module 35), which starts with correlations among variables and then builds a theory to explain them. Scores are collected on many interval level variables from a single group of people (or things) and their correlations are compared to what the correlations would be if the theory is correct. If the variables do correlate as expected, then the theory is *confirmed*. There are several statistics to choose from that indicate how well the correlations among the variables fit theoretical expectations. These are called *goodness-of-fit* statistics. As with other factor analysis approaches, it is not really the statistical significance of the statistics that leads to a conclusion about whether the data fit the model. Instead, it is often a matter of judging if the data fit a model "well enough" to stick with it.

This two-factor model with six variables expects this theoretical pattern for correlations.

Does this pattern of correlations from data collected in the real world fit the theory?

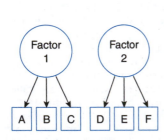

	A	B	C	D	E	F
A		1.00	1.00	.00	.00	.00
B			1.00	.00	.00	.00
C				.00	.00	.00
D					1.00	1.00
E						1.00
F						

	A	B	C	D	E	F
A		.82	.70	.10	.19	.15
B			.64	.11	.20	.12
C				.04	.12	.15
D					.86	.84
E						.78
F						

Primary Statistical Question

How well do the correlations among variables match theoretical expectations?

Example of a Study That Would Use Confirmatory Factor Analysis

Post-traumatic stress disorder (PTSD) is a condition that results from a strong emotional reaction to very stressful events. A common definition of PTSD includes these four characteristics: *emotional numbing, hyperarousal* (being "jumpy" or highly anxious), *reexperiencing* (constantly remembering or "reliving" the events), and *effortful avoidance* (avoiding reminders of the events). Researchers wanted to see which of two *models* of post-traumatic stress best explained the moderate correlations among these variables. A "one factor" model suggests the four variables represent a single "thing," *post-traumatic stress*. A "two factor" model suggests that *emotional numbing* and *hyperarousal* form an "emotional response" factor and *reexperiencing* and *effortful avoidance* form a kind of "cognitive-behavioral" factor that together define post-traumatic stress. They wondered which model fit the data better.

Analysis

The two competing models are shown graphically here:

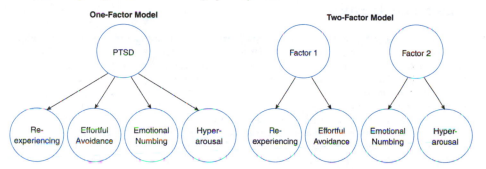

The actual measured correlations among the variables from a real-world sample of 524 people were calculated and compared to what each model said the correlations should be. From that comparison, and for each model, two goodness-of-fit indicator statistics were calculated from that comparison—a *chi-squared* and an RMSEA ("root mean square error of approximation"). For both statistics, *smaller* values indicate better fit. This table shows the goodness-of-fit values for the two models:

Model	Chi-Squared	RMSEA
One Factor	232.97	.045
Two Factors	242.89	.046

Both indicators were about the same for the two models, indicating that there was no meaningful difference between the two in terms of goodness of fit. Both models were equally confirmed. It may well be that there is really a single mental condition called post-traumatic stress disorder, or it might be that there are two different conditions that tend to coincide and together represent the disorder. The statistics won't help us figure out which one is best. Based on this data, the choice of one model as better than the other can be made only for theoretical reasons.

Real-Life Study That Inspired This Example

King, D. W., Leskin, G. A., King, L. A., & Weathers, F. W. (1998). Confirmatory factor analysis of the clinician-administered PTSD scale. *Psychological Assessment, 10*(2), 90–96.

Cluster Analysis

Predictor Variables	2+
Level of Measurement	Interval
Number of Levels	Many
Number of Groups	1
Criterion Variables	2+
Level of Measurement	Interval
Number of Levels	Many
Measurement Occasions	1

Research Design

If researchers know that an individual is a certain *type* of person or that the person has the same characteristics as some group, then it is easier to understand that person. That's why social science, and all of science, really, is eager to classify, categorize, and group people and things. It helps us understand the world around us. Sometimes, though, the best groups to use for whatever we are studying are not obvious. *Cluster analysis* is a statistical approach that groups people (or things) based on their similarities. Their similarities are shown in their scores on different interval level variables. It is a bit like exploratory factor analysis (see Module 35) that groups variables together based on similarities among the variables. Cluster analysis, though, groups people together based on similarities among people. Also, factor analysis gives us *loadings* to show how strongly a *variable* belongs on a *factor*, but cluster analysis gives us loadings for how strongly a *person* belongs in a *group*. While there are many strategies to identify "sameness" among a group of participants, a common approach uses *proximity*. The differences or distances between scores for all the grouping variables are standardized and analyzed statistically and usually displayed graphically. A simple cluster analysis shown here groups people based on their (nonstandardized) scores using two grouping variables.

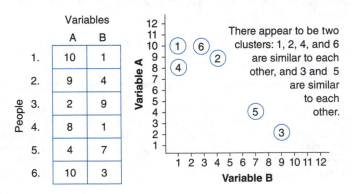

Primary Statistical Question

Based on their similarities, what is the best way to group people (or things)?

Example of a Study That Would Use Cluster Analysis

It is likely that investment fund managers who buy and sell stocks and bonds on behalf of clients have different styles and preferences. At least, a couple of researchers hypothesized as much and wondered whether managers could be grouped into different clusters based on the different styles. They used several interval level variables to perform a cluster analysis on a sample of 59 investment managers (representing 59 investment firms). The variables were measures of the nature of the stocks bought and held by the different managers and included scores indicating the extent to which the stocks had potential to increase in value, paid dividends, cost less than they were worth, were risky investments, and so on.

Analysis

Among the different possible ways for identifying clusters, this study looked at the correlation coefficients between all pairs of people on the variables to identify core pairs of managers whose styles were most similar. This first step initially defined the clusters. Then, an iterative process was used to refine the groupings until there were as few clusters as possible, while still maintaining a clear "distance" between groups.

At the conclusion of the cluster analysis process, there were two distinct groups that did a pretty good job of distinguishing 32 of the 59 managers, with most of the rest landing close to (sharing characteristics with) both clusters. By looking at the scores on the various descriptors of the stock portfolios in the two groups, the researchers were able to define and name two distinct styles of investment managers. The most common style (the cluster with the most members) was *Growth*. This style, reflected in about two-thirds of managers, buys the stocks of companies that they believe will grow faster than average in terms of earnings and revenue. The other style, preferred by about a third of the managers, was *Value*. This strategy involves finding and buying stocks that are undervalued and cost less than their fundamental worth using traditional formulas.

Things to Consider

There are many statistical ways to cluster people (or things) together. Researchers decide the grouping rules that make the most sense for their purpose.

If you have ever measured people on a variable and then placed them into groups based on their scores on that variable, you have performed a simple cluster analysis. Researchers do this all the time when they transform an interval level variable into a nominal level variable for some theoretical reason.

Cluster analysis is comparable to **discriminant analysis** (see Module 30), which classifies people into known groups. Cluster analysis, though, discovers possible groups and then classifies people into them.

For ease of discussion, statisticians refer to the "things" that will be classified in cluster analysis, whether they are people or minerals or events or whatever, as *objects*.

Cluster analysis is common in marketing research where it is used to identify types of consumers and place potential customers into demographic categories. One also often sees a cluster analysis strategy used in biology for developing classification systems.

Real-Life Study That Inspired This Example

Bailey, J. V., & Arnott, R. D. (1986). Cluster analysis and manager selection. *Financial Analysts Journal, 42*(6), 20–28.

Path Analysis

*When you wish to analyze
a chain of correlations among
several interval level variables*

Research Design

Path analysis is one of three correlational procedures intentionally placed together at the end of this book because it doesn't fit our simple predictors and criterion variables format. Like **structural equation modeling** (see Module 39) and **hierarchical linear modeling** (see Module 40), path analysis uses variables that, in the same analysis, act as *both* predictors and criterion variables. In path analysis, researchers identify correlations among pairs of interval level variables and build a connecting chain or path of relationships to understand how those variables work together. Essentially, path analysis defines a variable and builds a **simple linear regression** equation (see Module 32) to estimate that variable. Then, that variable becomes the predictor in another regression equation for a different variable. And so on. Path analysis examines those equations as a chain of **Pearson correlation coefficients** (see Module 31) or standardized regression weights.

The imagined path of relationships that explains a pattern of correlations is usually drawn as a picture with circles representing variables and the correlations between them shown as directional arrows. If there is a hypothesized relationship between a pair of variables, then an arrow is placed between them in the drawing. If there is no arrow between variables in the drawing, then the researcher believes there is not a relationship between them. The significance tests for path analysis apply to each individual correlation (or link in the chain) but also to the overall pattern of correlations and whether that pattern fits the theoretical expectations of some theory. In the real world, are there large correlations where there are arrows and low correlations where there are no arrows? That *goodness-of-fit* aspect of path analysis places it in the family of **confirmatory factor analyses** (see Module 36).

Linear Regression Equations Used to Model a Path of Relationships

Variable B = Variable A x (Standardized Weight)

Variable C = Variable B x (Standardized Weight)

Equations Shown as a Path of Correlations

A → .42 → B → .35 → C

Primary Statistical Question

How well does a theoretical model of relationships among variables match real-world correlations?

Example of a Study That Would Use Path Analysis

Researchers were interested in explaining performance in college math classes. Obviously, previous math experience or training (previous courses taken in college or high school) is probably a good predictor of college math performance, but they thought there was more to it than that. Their hypothesis was that the most direct influence on math performance was not previous training but mathematics *self-efficacy*. Self-efficacy is a type of confidence where people believe they can do what it takes to achieve a particular goal; the researchers thought that self-efficacy was determined by previous math experience. They theorized that self-efficacy, in turn, probably affected or explained a good "proportion of the variance" of college performance.

Analysis

In terms of a path model, the researchers' theory looked like the model on the left. After collecting data on 350 undergraduates and calculating the regression equations among all pairs of variables, they found the actual real-world set of weights for their path model shown on the right.

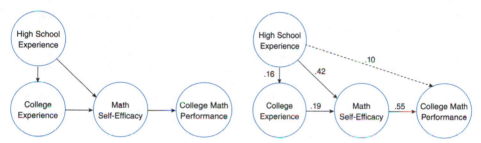

There were significant weights (relationships) between the variables as hypothesized. The strongest predictor of college math performance was self-efficacy, and the strongest predictor of self-efficacy was high school experience. An additional link, not theorized, found a weak but direct connection between high school experience and college math performance. This relationship existed above and beyond the "effects" of self-efficacy and previous college classes.

Things to Consider

- Path analysis is sometimes used to see if the correlation between two variables is explained by some third variable with which the first two variables are correlated. This third variable that accounts for a correlation like that is called a *mediator* because it is in the middle of the path diagram that would represent such a model.
- Because path analysis combines equations to build a model of relationships that can be tested for how well it fits a theory, it is a simple type of **structural equation modeling** (see Module 39).
- Correlations only show the strength of relationships, of course, not the direction of those relationships. Consequently, even though directional arrows are shown in paths and suggest a direction of influence or cause and effect, the correlations alone can seldom be used to verify the direction of a path. Theory must be used for that purpose.

Real-Life Study That Inspired This Example

Pajares, F., & Miller, M. D. (1994). Role of self-efficacy and self-concept beliefs in mathematical problem solving: A path analysis. *Journal of Educational Psychology, 86*(2), 193–203.

Structural Equation Modeling

When you wish to analyze a set of correlational chains and theoretical unmeasured variables

Research Design

Structural equation modeling (often called by its initials, SEM) is one of those flexible correlational procedures where the same variables can be both predictors and criterion in the same analysis. It is also a very broad and comprehensive analytic procedure that can describe and test models of relationships among variables that are measured directly and, also, those that are *latent variables* (hidden and only theoretically assumed variables sometimes called *factors*). It combines the goodness-of-fit strategies of **confirmatory factor analysis** (see Module 36) to define latent variables as some combination of measured variables, called *indicators*, with **path analysis** (see Module 38) to test hypotheses about how the latent variables are related.

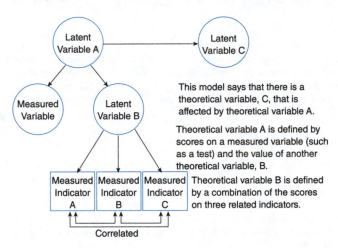

This model says that there is a theoretical variable, C, that is affected by theoretical variable A.

Theoretical variable A is defined by scores on a measured variable (such as a test) and the value of another theoretical variable, B.

Theoretical variable B is defined by a combination of the scores on three related indicators.

There are generally three statistical goals when analyzing the complex models that are tested using structural equation modeling:

- See how well real-world correlations among the measured and latent variables fit the expectations of a theoretical model.
- Calculate the strength of relationship between each pair of variables in the model (shown as weights on the linking arrows in the drawn model).
- If the sample size is very large, tinker with and "fine-tune" the theoretical model to improve the fit with real-world data.

Primary Statistical Question

How well do real-world correlations match a theoretical model?

Example of a Study That Would Use Structural Equation Modeling

Educational technology researchers had a theory about why people do or do not complete online degree programs. They thought that satisfaction with previous online experiences would predict continued participation, and they defined satisfaction as including six components related to expectations about the online experience. They theorized a model with the latent variable of *satisfaction* influencing *intention to continue with online learning*. To test their theory, they gathered data from 183 college students taking online courses. *Intention to continue* was gathered as an interval level measured variable. The latent variable *satisfaction* was defined as the combination of six indicators: *perceived usability, usability disconfirmation* (the difference between what was initially expected and current perception of usability), *perceived quality, quality disconfirmation, perceived value,* and *value disconfirmation*.

Analysis

A structural equation analysis on the real-world data provided some, but not complete, confirmation of the theoretical model. The results are shown here with standardized weights on each arrow indicating the relative strength of the relationships.

Overall fit was good (as judged by some statistical indices) and *satisfaction* was strongly related to *intention to continue*. In terms of defining satisfaction with those six components, *usability disconfirmation* was most important with the highest weight, followed by *perceived quality* and *value*.

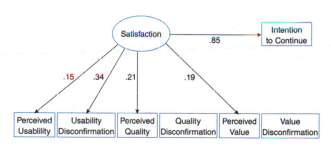

Two components, though, *quality disconfirmation* and *value disconfirmation*, did not appear to play a role in *satisfaction* (as indicated by the lack of arrows in the picture).

Things to Consider

- The term *structural equation modeling* covers any analysis that examines a network of relationships among variables, but it is usually reserved for complex cause-and-effect models that include latent variables, multiple links, and many hypothesized relationships.
- In structural equation models, latent variables are often shown as circles and measured variables or indicators are typically shown as squares.

Real-Life Study That Inspired This Example

Chiu, C., Hsu, M., Sun, S., Lin, T., & Sun, P. (2005). Usability, quality, value and e-learning continuance decisions. *Computers and Education, 45,* 399–416.

Hierarchical Linear Modeling

When you wish to control for the fact that your data are not independent of each other

Research Design

Hierarchical linear modeling (or HLM) is one of three complex correlational analyses placed at the end of this book because it doesn't fit nicely into a simple type of *independent and dependent variables* approach to design. HLM is designed to deal with a specific and tricky problem that sometimes arises in statistics. For statistical analyses to work correctly, a few assumptions about the data must be met. One assumption is that the data are *independent*. That means that the scores for any given variable produced by a participant in the study must be unrelated to any other partici-

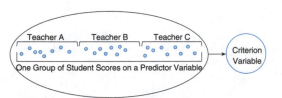

These predictor scores are related to the criterion variable. Each predictor score, though, is somewhat dependent on which classroom students are in. Hierarchical linear modeling calculates the relationship of the predictor with the criterion after controlling for the influence of theses unintended groupings.

pant's score. If scores on a variable are somehow influenced by other scores on the same variable, that assumption has been violated. If I collect scores measuring the attitude toward a political issue from 100 people, but some of those people are married to each other, I don't know whether to count those scores as 100 *independent* scores because spouses tend to have correlated attitudes. Another example is in educational research, where participants are often already "nested" into classrooms with several subgroups of students all being influenced by a few different teachers. Imagine that I have collected reading scores from 40 fifth graders to see what influence parents' income has on reading, but those 40 students actually come from only three different classrooms. Students in the same classroom tend to score somewhat the same on reading tests because they have been taught by the same teacher. Hierarchical linear modeling identifies that type of dependency in your data and controls for it. This way, you can see the clean relationship between some variable and another *as if* the scores on the predictor variable were all independent.

Primary Statistical Question

What is the relationship among variables after controlling for dependency in the data?

Example of a Study That Would Use Hierarchical Linear Modeling

Evaluators of an intervention designed to lower aggressive behavior in the classroom studied 6,715 students across the United States and scored their behavior (the dependent variable) based on whether their classroom did or did not receive the intervention (the independent variable). Because classroom environments have an effect on student behavior, hierarchical linear regression was conducted, controlling for *students nested in classrooms*.

Analysis

The first step was to see if, in fact, the classroom variable was related to aggressive behavior. It was. The next step, then, was to see if the two groups of the independent variable differed on the dependent variable after controlling for the influence of differing classrooms on that effect. They did. HLM uses regression for its analysis, and a final complex regression equation (which actually includes a separate regression equation for each classroom within it) provides a standardized weight for the independent variable describing its relationship with the criterion. That weight is tested statistically. For this study the weight was significant ($p = .03$) and represented about a .20 standard deviation benefit for those students who received the intervention. This was interpreted as a small to moderate effect of the intervention on aggression.

Things to Consider

- In repeated measures, scores at each point are dependent on (correlated with) the scores from the previous point. This is dependency, so HLM is sometimes used to explore changes across time with what is called *growth curve analysis*.
- In HLM, there are different levels of relationships, with lower-level scores nested within higher levels. Most analyses have two or, sometimes, three levels, but there can be more.
- It is easy to give HLM examples that talk about educational research, but controlling for dependency in your data can be done in any field.
- In hierarchical linear modeling, we often talk of hierarchies with students in groups. These groups are not the same "groups" as we use in analysis of variance where different levels of a nominal independent variable create different groups of scores.
- *HLM* has become the common way to describe this statistical approach partly because there is a popular software package for the analysis with that name. The more generic term for this type of analysis is *multilevel modeling*.
- Both the terms *independent-dependent* variables and *predictor-criterion* variables are used in our discussion of this analysis because HLM can be used with both experimental and correlational designs.
- With its complex mix of regression models, hierarchical linear modeling is similar to **structural equation modeling** (see Module 39). In fact, both analytic approaches can be used to solve many of the same problems, and HLM is really a type of SEM.

Real-Life Study That Inspired This Example

CPPR Group. (1999). Initial impact of the Fast Track prevention trial for conduct problems: II. Classroom effects. *Journal of Consulting and Clinical Psychology, 67*(5), 648–657.

Index